The European Constitution

by

Jacques Ziller

preface by

Giuliano Amato

translated by

Mel Marquis

A C.I.P. catalogue record for this book is available from the Library of Congress.

ISBN 90-411-2395-4

Published by:
Kluwer Law International
P.O. Box 85889
2508 CN The Hague
The Netherlands

Sold and distributed in North, Central and South America by:
Aspen Publishers, Inc.
7201 McKinney Circle
Frederick, MD 21704
USA

Sold and distributed in all other countries by:
Extenza-Turpin Distribution Services
Stratton Business Park
Pegasus Drive
Biggleswade
Bedfordshire SG18 8TQ
United Kingdom

Printed on acid-free paper

© Éditions La Découverte, Paris, France, 2004
Translated by Mel Marquis from the French original 'La Nouvelle Constitution Européenne'.

Printed in The Netherlands

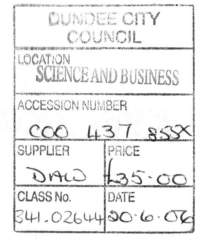

To D.U.,
With all my love

TABLE OF CONTENTS

PREFACE

Jacques Ziller has profound expertise in the areas of constitutional law and governmental systems. Yet he does not wrap himself in the obscure language of the specialist, which so frequently alienates those not initiated in the arcane rites of the subject. To the contrary, Ziller writes in a manner that is clear, simple and captivating for all audiences. And the value of his works resides not only in the language he uses but also in the architecture of their design, which simplifies the subjects he engages and sheds light on their fundamental features. In this way, Professor Ziller spares the reader from having to meander through excessive technicalities, which are often no more than a playground where the *legalese* of jurists runs amok.

Such is the mark of the present work, in which Ziller has devoted his attention to the European Convention, the draft Constitutional Treaty it proposed to the European Council, the final result, i.e., the "Treaty establishing a Constitution for Europe", subsequently adopted by the heads of State and government, and the ratification process currently underway. Professor Ziller has thus rendered a service of inestimable value, to the benefit of the Convention and the Constitution itself, for which I must express my gratitude.

The Convention was born from a need to give the European Union a breath of democracy, as it were, as the Union had been suffering increasingly from a lack of oxygen caused by the gap between its Institutions and its citizens. And what we accomplished at the Convention to simplify the Union's legal instruments and procedures, clarify the allocation of competences, and create more open and practicable means of access for national parliaments and citizens' organisations is aimed precisely at fulfilling that need. At the same time, however, it must be acknowledged that the Convention was also a *product* of that ivory-tower Europe which seemed so distant from the citizenry. And although the Convention succeeded as far as possible in bridging the gap thanks both to the transparent and public nature of its proceedings and to the involvement of many segments of "civil society", not only do many Europeans remain oblivious to the Convention, but even those who *have* heard of it know little about the contents of the Convention's text and their meaning. Yet nothing could be more helpful in this regard than conscientious works such as the present one, in which Ziller's writing will undoubtedly sustain the interest of readers from the first page to the last (unusual as that may be for a book!). I trust and hope that this work will serve as a model in the coming months for those who report and comment on the subject, not only in the written press, but also in other media, to make clearer to Europeans the changes affecting them.

In the pages that follow there is an answer to all the questions and all of the curiosity that one might have about the Convention, about the draft Constitution it produced, and about the differences between that text and the one finally adopted by the Member State governments. Ziller's book thus contains practically everything there is to know about what the Convention *was*: its background, its composition and internal organisation, how the work was carried out, the political affiliation of its members, the characteristics and quality of the Secretariat, and the profile of the principal players, including even the three solitary champions of "anti-Europeanism" – Bonde from Denmark, the Frenchman Abitbol, and Heathcoat-Amory of the UK.

Further, one finds in this book everything there is to know about what the Convention *did*. Here too there is the background, the progress of the work from the simplification of the Treaties to the drafting of a text bearing the name of a Constitution, its chapters and themes, the problems addressed by each of them, the major objections made to the text, and the results achieved. Moreover – and this is one of the book's most extraordinary features – Ziller's commentary is regularly accompanied by tables illustrating essential terms and concepts pertinent to the discussion. For example, when the discussion refers to the method for calculating a majority vote on the basis of the number of Member States and the number of each State's inhabitants, there is a table indicating Member State populations and thus of the weight accorded to each State's vote. When the subject is the Charter of Human Rights and Fundamental Freedoms, there is a table comparing the rights conferred by the Charter with those established by the Americans in the Constitution of the United States. Likewise, the description of the various configurations of the Council of Ministers is supplemented by a table depicting such configurations one by one. Indeed, where the official languages of the Constitution are discussed, there is not only a list of the 21 languages in which it is written but also a synoptic table containing key passages in the languages of the four largest Member States (i.e., French, English, German and Italian) and indicating certain differences (at times not merely a question of nuances) that arise when passing from one language to another. So abundant is this kind of supplementary information that I am certain the book will be extremely useful – not only for non-specialists but indeed for seasoned experts, who may well find things in Ziller's text that are too embarrassing to be asked but in many cases too little known.

The results of the Convention are portrayed in a spirit that exalts the constitutional potential of the "Convention method" yet maintains a healthy realism regarding its complexity. Ziller also refers to my personal quarrel with the text – i.e., that we sired a "boy" (since *trattato*, the word for "treaty" in Italian, takes a masculine gender) whereas I had been hoping for a "girl" (i.e., a true *Costituzione*) – yet he rightly concludes that the international nature of the procedure for future amendments (which had prompted me to make my *trattato* remark) does not preclude it, thanks to its substance, from achieving the rank of a true Constitution. Indeed, as Ziller explains, the Constitution is structured according to the classic canons of the post-French Revolution constitutions (i.e., proceeding from a recognition of the rights of citizens to the organisation of the relationships between the government and the governed, and then to guarantees of rights and powers). And the incorporation of the Charter, despite the tiresome compromises exacted by the British delegates as a condition for acceptance, is one of the spectacular successes of the Convention.

In terms of his final verdict, Ziller shares (with good reason, I believe) that of Convention President Valéry Giscard d'Estaing: *"Imparfaite, mais inespérée"* ("Imperfect, but beyond what could have been hoped for".) Keenly aware of the history of the EU, Ziller knows how many taboos were broken by the Convention and is able (with fitting sobriety) to appreciate the changes that have been achieved more fully than those who may approach the subject on the basis of more specific, often very lofty objectives. The *proper* comparison, as Ziller observes, is by reference to the Convention's *precedents*, rather than to each person's individual expectations. In addition, the fact that a ready-to-use *constitutional text* emerged from the Convention – on the basis of a mandate that spoke merely of "recommendations" – could scarcely have been expected. The Convention certainly cannot therefore be faulted for a lack of audacity! On the other hand, a greater degree of qualified majority voting would not have hurt. And Ziller is critical of the failure to insert, as one of the Union's basic legal instruments, the "organic" laws known to many national legal systems. Furthermore, many of the novelties introduced in the Constitution beg a number of questions. What, for example, will be the stature of the President of the European Council? Will he be a President *all'italiana*, or *à la française*?

In considering such questions, it is useful to refer to Ziller's conclusions. The Convention opened amidst long-standing questions that had never been answered unambiguously: Is Europe to be a federal *State* – or a confederation? Will Europe remain the Europe that put its faith in the Convention, or will it expand yet again? To these questions the Convention did not provide answers. Yet one senses that, according to Ziller, the Convention did well not to go down that road. The Constitution we drafted is a Constitution for a mathematical "open set" – open in terms of its borders and open in the institutional forms that will be able to take shape in the future on the basis of its new dictates. Not even the revolutionary constitutions (we have come to realise) represent total caesuras with respect to past history – nor do they paint in the details of the future.

Of course, the Constitution that is now proceeding through the ratification stage (involving the parliaments and, in many cases, the citizens themselves by way of

referendums) is less open than that of the Convention and rather more characteristic of the ways of the past. No longer counterbalanced by the European and
national parliaments, which at the Convention had expressed visions far removed
from narrow national interests, the Member State governments unfortunately
reintroduced unanimous voting requirements, thus reclaiming sole authority over
matters the Convention had proposed to entrust to the co-decision procedure
(which would have involved the European Parliament). In other respects too the
Member States have sacrificed, for the sake of their own interests, the efficiency
and flexibility of many of the Convention's proposed solutions. Be that as it may,
in assessing the Constitution's future it remains only to concur with Ziller's own
conclusions: First, it is hoped that the ratification process will succeed because, if
it does not, this will mean victory for "anti-Europeanism" and a defeat for
the prospects of a better Europe. Then, once past that hurdle, the Constitution will
be something to be lived and experienced, knowing that it will give all of us the
opportunity to draw on it and to use it to build Europe's future history.

Our first responsibility is to familiarise ourselves as far as possible with the
new Constitution – and we are supremely well poised to do this thanks to this
superb contribution of Jacques Ziller.

Giuliano Amato
Vice-President of the European Convention, 2002–2003

NOTE REGARDING CITATIONS

Citations to the Treaty establishing a Constitution for Europe are excerpted from the final version of the text. A provisional version of the Constitution was published on 6 August 2004, following which a number of minor corrigenda were adopted. A slightly revised version of the text dated 13 October 2004 was then made available and this final version of the Constitution was signed in Rome on 29 October 2004. Subsequently the Constitution was also published in the Official Journal of the European Union (OJ 2004 C310/3). The final text is available on the internet site of the Council of the European Union at http://ue.eu.int.

References to the "Convention's text" correspond to Document CONV 850/03, which is available on the internet site of the European Convention at http://european-convention.eu.int/ and which was published in the Official Journal (OJ 2003 C169/01) on 18 July 2003.

The reader's attention is drawn to the fact that, in the Convention's text, the Articles contained in Part I of the Constitution were numbered exclusively in Arabic numerals, whereas those of Parts II, III and IV were preceded by the Roman numerals II, III and IV respectively (e.g., "Article III-50"). In addition, in each of Parts II, III and IV the Arabic numbering began anew. For example, there is an "Article II-1", an "Article III-1" and an "Article IV-1". By contrast, the definitive text of the Constitution contains a continuous progression of Arabic numerals from beginning to end, each proceeded by the appropriate Roman numeral (including a Roman numeral I for the Articles in Part I). For example, the first Article in Part II is not "Article II-1" but Article "II-61".

Citations to provisions in the Treaties of Rome and Maastricht are those applying after the entry into force of the Treaty of Nice, i.e., the current numbering is used. However, the current numbers are followed by an "ex-Art. XX" in order to indicate the corresponding provisions as they were known prior to the renumbering of the Treaties on the occasion of the Treaty of Amsterdam.

Abbreviations used in this book

CFSP	Common Foreign and Security Policy
COREPER	Committee of Permanent Representatives
CFI	European Court of First Instance

ECSC	European Coal and Steel Community
ECHR	European Convention on Human Rights
ECJ	European Court of Justice
EDC	European Defence Community
EEA	European Economic Area
EEC	European Economic Community
EFTA	European Free Trade Association
EU	European Union
EUI	European University Institute (Florence)
Euratom	European Atomic Energy Community
IGC	Intergovernmental Conference
JHA	Justice and Home Affairs

WHY *HAVE* A CONSTITUTION?

1. WHAT HAS CHANGED? A CONSTITUTION IN THE TRADITION OF THE ENLIGHTENMENT

On 18 July 2003, the President of the European Convention, Valéry Giscard d'Estaing, presented the complete text of the *Draft Treaty Establishing a Constitution for Europe* to Silvio Berlusconi, who was acting as President of the European Council for the second half of 2003. During the press conference at which this transfer took place, a fly hovered in the air near Giscard, apparently seeking to interrupt him just as he began explaining to the public the opposition to the Constitution on the part of the so-called "Eurosceptics". At the precise moment at which the fly lighted in front of him, Berlusconi took the bound volume that had just been given to him and flattened the insect with a sharp and lethal blow. With a wry smile, Giscard quipped: "There, we have the first victim of the European Constitution!" It may well be that Giscard's joke pre-empted what otherwise could have been an easy (although inappropriate) remark about the utility of a text which *The Economist* had recommended tossing in the rubbish scarcely a month before. The events that followed demonstrated that it was easier to kill a fly than to convince the other 24 heads of State and government to approve some of the innovations that the Convention had proposed. In the end, however, on 18 June 2004, Irish Prime Minister Bertie Ahern succeeded where Berlusconi had failed.

The draft prepared by the Convention was, from the beginning – and will continue to be in the future – the object of reflections and commentaries of politicians and jurists, whose criticisms will undoubtedly take aim at targets other than innocuous insects. But in any event it is necessary to find an answer to the fundamental question, namely: Of what *use* is a European Constitution?

Preface to the Convention's Text

Noting that the European Union was coming to a turning point in its existence, the European Council which met in Laeken, Belgium, on 14 and 15 December 2001 convened the European Convention on the Future of Europe.

The Convention was asked to draw up proposals on three subjects: how to bring citizens closer to the European design and European Institutions; how to organise politics and the European political area in an enlarged Union; and how to develop the Union into a stabilising factor and a model in the new world order.

The Convention has identified responses to the questions put in the Laeken declaration:
– it proposes a better division of Union and Member State competences;
– it recommends a merger of the Treaties and the attribution of legal personality to the Union;
– it establishes a simplification of the Union's instruments of action;
– it proposes measures to increase the democracy, transparency and efficiency of the European Union, by developing the contribution of national Parliaments to the legitimacy of the European design, by simplifying the decision-making processes, and by making the functioning of the European Institutions more transparent and comprehensible;
– it establishes the necessary measures to improve the structure and enhance the role of each of the Union's three institutions, taking account, in particular, of the consequences of enlargement.

The Laeken declaration also asked whether the simplification and reorganisation of the Treaties should not pave the way for the adoption of a constitutional text. The Convention's proceedings ultimately led to the drawing up of a draft Treaty establishing a Constitution for Europe, which achieved a broad consensus at the plenary session on 13 June 2003.

That is the text which it is our privilege to present today, 20 June 2003, to the European Council meeting in Thessaloniki, on behalf of the European Convention, in the hope that it will constitute the foundation of a future Treaty establishing the European Constitution.

Valéry Giscard d'Estaing, President of the Convention

Giuliano Amato, Vice-President

Jean-Luc Dehaene, Vice-President

The constitutional tradition of Western democracies derives in large part from the Constitution of the United States of 1787 and from the French Revolution of 1789. Although its roots can be traced back to ancient Greece, and although it owes much to the English revolutions of the 17th Century, it is above all a product of the Century of the Enlightenment. The Western constitutional tradition is founded on the ideas of the 18th Century philosophers according to which a constitution should fulfil three essential functions. In particular, it should provide for: a recognition of the rights of citizens; the organisation of the relations between the government and the governed; and a system of checks and balances among the branches of the government, e.g., between the legislative and executive branches. The Constitution is, in other words, a *Social Contract*, even though social contracts are normally concluded within the context of a State.

Article 16 of the French Declaration of the Rights of Man and of the Citizen, which was proclaimed in August of 1789, states: "Any society in which the guarantee of rights is not secured, and in which the separation of powers is not determined, has no constitution at all."

The draft Constitution adopted by the European Convention in two consecutive sessions (on 13 June 2003 for Parts I and II, and on 10 July 2003 for Parts III and IV), which was later modified in part by the Intergovernmental Conference (IGC) and finally approved on 18 June 2004, cannot be fully appreciated from an abstract reading. Indeed, the Convention did not make a *tabula rasa* of the past; on the contrary, it inscribed its work within the continuity of the European integration effort.

Put briefly, the European Constitution represents an extension of the Declaration of Robert Schuman of 9 May 1950, a date which by no coincidence is recalled by Article I-8: "Europe day shall be celebrated on 9 May throughout the Union." In his Declaration, Schuman, who was at that time the French Minister of Foreign Affairs, proposed that France and Germany – although the invitation was extended to all countries that desired to participate – should pool their respective means of production of coal and steel: "[T]here will be realised simply and speedily that fusion of interests which is indispensable to the establishment of a common economic system; it may be the leaven from which may grow a wider and deeper community between countries long opposed to one another by bloody conflicts. . . . [T]his proposal will lead to the realisation of the first concrete foundation of a European federation indispensable to the preservation of peace."

It is both inevitable and legitimate that every reader will judge the text elaborated by the Convention of 2003, as modified and adopted by the heads of State and government in 2004, by weighing it on the basis of his or her own hopes and fears and by reference to the initial European project. However, the most precise way to evaluate the utility of the constitutional project of 2003-2004 is not so much by comparing it to the original idea but rather by considering it in light of the realities of the debut of the 21st Century. More particularly, the most relevant comparisons are those to be made with the two main existing Treaties, the EC Treaty (i.e., the Treaty of Rome) and the Treaty on European Union (i.e., the Treaty of Maastricht).

1.1. The Protection of Human Rights.

1.1.1. The Charter of Fundamental Rights of the European Union

All the constitutions of the Member States of the European Union (including the 10 Member States that joined the Union on 1 May 2004) contain, in one form or another, a declaration of fundamental rights. Even in the United Kingdom, which does not have a *written* constitution, there is nevertheless a *Bill of Rights*, dating back to 1689 and finally completed in 1999. The European Convention for the Protection of Human Rights and Fundamental Freedoms, which was signed in Rome on 4 November 1950 and which entered into force on 3 September 1953, was ratified by all of the member countries of the Council of Europe (46 as of 2005) and, in particular, by all of the Member States of the Union.

The underlying foundations of the European Communities, which were essentially economic in origin, clearly explains the lack of a declaration of rights in the Treaty of Paris (1951) and the Treaty of Rome (1957). However, ever since the Treaty of Maastricht (1992) introduced the concept of EU citizenship, the absence of such a declaration has underlined the limits of this new concept.

Against this background, a first Convention gathered in 1999-2000 and prepared a Charter of Fundamental Rights of the European Union. The Charter did not create

3

new rights but rather enshrined, in a solemn manner, a whole series of rights and principles that only legal experts had been able to draw from the Treaties, from Community directives and regulations, and most importantly from the case law of the European Court of Justice. Yet several of the governments among the then-15 Member States strongly opposed the idea of making the Charter legally binding. Some of these governments objected under the pretext that the Charter included certain social rights which, they maintained, were incompatible with the efficient functioning of the market, or due to fears of budgetary consequences. Other governments argued, to the contrary, that the Charter did not go far *enough* in protecting certain rights and were concerned that the Charter would be used to compel them to limit their systems of social protection and welfare. This explains why the Charter was merely "signed and proclaimed", a formality conducted at the summit of the Intergovernmental Conference (IGC) in Nice on 7 December 2000 by the Presidents of the European Parliament, the Commission and the European Council.

However, the working methods of the Convention of 2002-2003 proved successful where those of the IGC of 2000 had not: one of the spectacular results of the Convention was that it conferred legal force on the Charter, incorporating it as Part II of the Constitution. What has changed, with the inclusion of the Charter in the Constitution, is, first of all, the Charter's visibility. It was not by coincidence that the President of the Convention presented the first two Parts of the draft Constitution together to the European Council of Thessaloniki on 20 June 2003. Indeed, Parts I and II represent the heart of the Constitution, and they have been published and made available as a single document, notably in the European press.

The other thing that has changed is that all of the Institutions of the Union will be legally obliged to respect the Charter, as will the governments, parliaments and administrations of the Member States when they are implementing Union law. The Commission, in proposing legislative texts, and the European Parliament and the Council of Ministers in approving or amending those texts, may do so only within the limits imposed by the rights inscribed in the Charter.

If individuals (regardless of whether they are citizens of the Union), or if companies or associations consider that their rights have been infringed by EU legislation, or by national implementing legislation, they will be able to bring legal proceedings before a court and seek remedies for the failure to respect such rights. The same will apply in respect of decisions taken by the Commission or by the national authorities in application of EU law.

Community law specialists have been pondering, since December of 2000, whether and to what extent the Charter can modify the substance of EU law, given that the original Charter essentially "codified" principles that could already be found in the case law of the European Courts and in other relevant sources. Yet these musings seem likely to be overtaken by the fact that, in practice, thousands of lawyers and judges who may not be EU law experts will be able to refer to a text that is much more accessible than the case law of the European Courts and the vertiginous debates in the pages of law journals. And it seems fair to predict that this enhanced accessibility will lead to greater effectiveness in the protection of rights.

Furthermore, given that it is now an integral part of the Constitution, one may assume that the Charter will also be read by non-lawyers, teachers, journalists, interest groups, etc. Indeed, a reading of the Charter, the Preamble to the Constitution, and the Articles in Part I concerning the values and objectives of the Union (i.e., Articles I-2 and I-3) may well be the first step towards a common culture of EU citizenship.

1.1.2. The Values of the European Union

A relatively new polemic is stirring public opinion in certain Member States, especially in Italy and Poland, and much to the delight of the national and international press, which stokes the debate with headlines such as: "No place for God in the Constitution." The issue is whether it is appropriate to include a reference in the Constitution to religion and, in particular, to Christianity. This controversy is potentially of great importance, considering the diverse conceptions in the Member States regarding the relationship between Church and State: for example, secularism and a total separation between Church and State are fundamental legal principles in France, whereas in England, the Queen is the head of the Anglican Church, and in Germany, priests, pastors and rabbis receive payment from the State. Furthermore, the clout of Islamic populations in France and the UK in particular have made the political parties in these countries sensitive to the impact of national policies and to the potential risk that such policies may give rise to feelings of exclusion in relation to the overall national community.

European Constitution, Article I-2

The Union's Values

The Union is founded on the values of respect for human dignity, freedom, democracy, equality, the rule of law and respect for human rights, including the rights of persons belonging to minorities. These values are common to the Member States in a society in which pluralism, non-discrimination, tolerance, justice, solidarity and equality between women and men prevail.

Giuliano Amato, one of the two Vice-Presidents of the Convention (along with Jean-Luc Dehaene) focused his attention on this issue and sought to explain to the public that the function of Article I-2 was meant to be a standard against which to measure the respect of the Member States for common values, and that this standard was reinforced elsewhere in the Constitution (Article I-59) by sanctions in case of a violation. It would therefore be inappropriate in that provision to make any reference to God or religion. On the other hand, Article II-70 in fact guarantees freedom of religion while Article I-52 ensures respect for the status, provided for under national law, of churches and religious associations and communities in the Member States. Once this was understood, the debate shifted to the Constitution's Preamble. After several drafts, the Praesidium (i.e., the group responsible for actually writing the Convention's text) finally reached a solution that seemed acceptable to the various interests concerned: the final draft refers to the "cultural, religious and humanist inheritance of Europe", but not to Europe's Christian roots. It is worth noting that the majority of constitutions in European countries, as well as that of the United States, follow the same approach, i.e., they remain silent concerning particular religious affiliations.

Part II of the Constitution – Charter of Fundamental Rights of the Union

---

Preamble

The peoples of Europe, in creating an ever closer union among them, are resolved to share a peaceful future based on common values.

Conscious of its spiritual and moral heritage, the Union is founded on the indivisible, universal values of human dignity, freedom, equality and solidarity; it is based on the principles of democracy and the rule of law. It places the individual at the heart of its activities, by establishing the citizenship of the Union and by creating an area of freedom, security and justice.

The Union contributes to the preservation and to the development of these common values while respecting the diversity of the cultures and traditions of the peoples of Europe as well as the national identities of the Member States and the organisation of their public authorities at national, regional and local levels; it seeks to promote balanced and sustainable development and ensures free movement of persons, services, goods and capital, and the freedom of establishment.

To this end, it is necessary to strengthen the protection of fundamental rights in the light of changes in society, social progress and scientific and technological developments by making those rights more visible in a Charter.

This Charter reaffirms, with due regard for the powers and tasks of the Union and the principle of subsidiarity, the rights as they result, in particular, from the constitutional traditions and international obligations common to the Member States, the European Convention for the Protection of Human Rights and Fundamental Freedoms, the Social Charters adopted by the Union and by the Council of Europe and the case law of the Court of Justice of the European Union and of the European Court of Human Rights. In this context the Charter will be interpreted by the courts of the Union and the Member States with due regard to the explanations prepared under the authority of the Praesidium of the Convention which drafted the Charter and updated under the responsibility of the Praesidium of the European Convention.

Enjoyment of these rights entails responsibilities and duties with regard to other persons, to the human community and to future generations.

The Union therefore recognises the rights, freedoms and principles set out hereafter.

1.1.3. Fundamental Rights in Part II of the Constitution

One of the most frequently raised criticisms of the Charter is that it gives citizens of the Union false impressions, leading them to believe that the rights contained in the Charter protect them whatever the circumstances, as is the case in the Member States by virtue of their respective constitutions, or in the US by virtue of the well-known amendments to its federal constitution. In reality, the Charter is addressed

critique

in the first instance only to the Institutions of the Union (i.e., the European Parliament, the Commission, the European Council, the Council of Ministers and the Court of Justice) and to the Union's bodies, offices and agencies. By contrast, with respect to the Member States, Article II-111 limits the application of the Charter to situations in which they are implementing Union (as opposed to strictly national) law.

The difference can be illustrated by considering Article II-62 (*Right to life*), which, after providing that "[e]veryone has the right to life", specifies that "[n]o one shall be condemned to the death penalty, or executed". Critics relish pointing out that, since the Union does not have police, criminal courts, prisons or executioners, the prohibition against capital punishment is scarcely of any consequence. However, there are two ways in which this provision is capable of having concrete effects. Firstly, it seems clear that the Union could not accept among its ranks a Member State that administered the death penalty. Indeed, if a Member State adopted (or re-established) capital punishment, it would almost certainly be subject to the sanction contained in Article I-59 (*Suspension of certain rights resulting from Union membership*). Secondly, in a more complex and indirect sense, the content of Article II-62 could play an important role in the relations between the Union and third countries, for example, as a justification for the use of commercial sanctions that would otherwise be contrary to the Union's economic interests.

Beyond their more immediate and practical consequences, the *symbolic* aspect of the values espoused in the Constitution is fundamental. And these values compare quite favourably with those embraced in the most famous of the modern constitutions, that of the United States. To be fair, many of the differences between the two texts may be explained by the 225 years that separate them, and by the fact that the practical importance attached to fundamental rights on the two sides of the Atlantic often vary. Nevertheless, in some cases the differences are particularly revealing because they highlight significant divergences in values. For example, the prohibition in Article II-62 against the death penalty is in stark contrast to the laws of 38 of the states in the US. And the Second Amendment to the US Constitution, which provides for the right to bear arms, is simply unimaginable in Europe.

Fundamental Rights in the European and US Constitutions

European Constitution (2003-04)	US Constitution (1787)
Article II-61: Human dignity	
No equivalent	2nd Amendment (1789-91): Right to bear arms
Article II-62: Right to life	*The US Supreme Court does not consider the death penalty to be cruel and unusual punishment under the 8th Amendment*
Article II-63: Right to the integrity of the person	

Fundamental Rights in the European and US Constitutions (Cont'd)

European Constitution (2003-04)	US Constitution (1787)
Article II-64: Prohibition of torture and inhuman or degrading treatment or punishment	8th Amendment (1789-91)
Article II-65: Prohibition of slavery and forced labour	13th Amendment (1865)
Article II-66: Right to liberty and security	4th Amendment (1789-91): Unreasonable searches and seizures
Article II-67: Respect for private and family life; II-68 and I-51: Protection of personal data; II-69: Right to marry and right to found a family	4th Amendment (1789-91): Right to privacy said to "emanate" from this provision
Article II-70: Freedom of thought, conscience and religion	1st Amendment (1789-91)
Article II-71: Freedom of expression and information	*Idem*
Article II-72: Freedom of assembly and of association	*Idem*
Article II-73: Freedom of the arts and sciences; II-74:Right to education; II-75: Freedom to choose an occupation and right to engage in work; II-76: Freedom to conduct a business	
Article II-77: Right to property	5th Amendment (1789-91): Takings Clause (right to just compensation); 3d Amendment (1789-91): Quartering of troops in time of war
Article II-78: Right to asylum; II-79: Protection in the event of removal, expulsion or extradition	
Article II-80: Equality before the law	14th Amendment (1868) and 15th Amendment (1870): Equal Protection Clause (interpretation extended in the second half of the 20th Century
Article II-81: Non-discrimination	*Idem*
Article II-82: Cultural, religious and linguistic diversity	
Article II-83: Equality between women and men	19th Amendment (1920): Universal suffrage (Right to vote granted to women)
Article II-84: The rights of the child; II-85: The rights of the elderly; II-86: Integration of persons with disabilities	
Article II-87: Workers' right to information and consultation within the undertaking; II-88: Right of collective bargaining and action; II-89: Right of access to placement services; II-90: Protection in the event of unjustified	

Fundamental Rights in the European and US Constitutions (Cont'd)

European Constitution (2003-04)	US Constitution (1787)
dismissal; II-91: Fair and just working conditions; II-92: Prohibition of child labour and protection of young people at work; II-93: Family and professional life; II-94: Social security and social assistance; II-95: Health care; II-96: Access to services of general economic interest; II-97: Environmental protection; II-98: Consumer protection	
Articles II-99 and I-10: Right to vote and to stand as a candidate at elections to the European Parliament; II-100 and I-10: Right to vote and to stand as a candidate at municipal elections	
Article II-101: Right to good administration; I-102: Right of access to documents; II-103 and I-10: European Ombudsman	
Articles II-104 and I-10: Right to petition	1st Amendment (1789-91)
Articles II-105 and I-10: Freedom of movement and of residence	Article 4, Sec. 2: Privileges and Immunities Clause (construed as implying a right of interstate travel)
Articles II-106 and I-10: Diplomatic and consular protection	
Article II-107: Right to an effective remedy and to a fair trial	4th, 5th and 6th Amendments (1789-91)
Article II-108: Presumption of innocence and right of defence	4th, 5th and 6th Amendments (1789-91): Presumption of innocence said to be implied by these provisions; Article 1, Sec. 9: *habeas corpus*
Article II-109: Principles of legality and proportionality of criminal offences and penalties	Article 1, Sec. 9: Prohibition against retroactive (*ex post facto*) penalties
Article II-110: Right not to be tried or punished twice in criminal proceedings for the same criminal offence	5th Amendment (1789-91): Double Jeopardy
No equivalent	7th Amendment (1789-91): Right to a jury in civil matters
Article II-112: Scope and interpretation of rights and principles	9th Amendment (1789-91): Non-regression Clause (rights explicitly guaranteed do not deny or disparage others not mentioned)
Article II-113: Level of protection	*Idem*
Article II-114: Prohibition of abuse of rights	
Article I-11: Fundamental principles (competences of the Union); principle of conferral	10th Amendment (1789-91): Powers not delegated to Congress reserved to the states or to the people

1.2. A Clearer Separation of Powers

The Declaration of the Rights of Man and of the Citizen, adopted in 1789, attaches the same importance to the separation of powers and the protection of fundamental rights. The Declaration does not specify what is meant by the "separation of powers", but it refers implicitly to the classical division of powers described by Montesquieu in his famous work, *L'Esprit des lois* ("The Spirit of Laws"). This familiar allocation of powers is common to all pluralist democracies and on the one hand distinguishes between the legislative, executive and judicial functions, while on the other hand proscribing the concentration of these functions in the hands of a single person or institution. One rather simplistic but widely practiced variant of this concept is one in which each branch or institution is distinct and independent but is endowed with certain core powers that may be exercised against the others: the parliament is given legislative powers and the government is vested with executive powers while the judiciary role is assigned to tribunals. The reality is that in all pluralist democracies, the parliament (or legislature) and the government each participate, albeit in different ways, in the exercise of both the legislative and executive functions. However, the separation between the two institutions is symbolised by the fact that it is the parliament that has the last word in relation to the adoption of national laws, while the government is charged with administering such laws, under the political control of the parliament and the juridical control of the courts.

The European Constitution introduces two changes worth noting which help to clarify the separation of powers among the Institutions of the Union. These changes are far from radical, and indeed their impact is relatively limited by the fact that the "Community method" (explained below at pages 21–24) – which attributes a very stylised role to the European Commission – has been maintained. Still, the importance of these innovations should not be underestimated.

1.2.1. European Laws and Regulations
One consequence of the separation of powers in pluralist democracies is the distinction made between laws, which are acts of parliament, and regulations, which are acts of the government (which may consist of, for example, federal regulations or *executive orders* in the US, or *orders in Council* in the UK). The European Constitution re-establishes this distinction, which is totally absent in the Treaties of Rome and Maastricht. This is one of the most visible results of the Convention's efforts to simplify and clarify the Treaties.

European Constitution, Article I-33

The Legal Acts of the Union

1. To exercise the Union's competences the institutions shall use as legal instruments, in accordance with Part III, European laws, European framework laws, European regulations, European decisions, recommendations and opinions.

A European law shall be a legislative act of general application. It shall be binding in its entirety and directly applicable in all Member States.

A European framework law shall be a legislative act binding, as to the result to be achieved, upon each Member State to which it is addressed, but shall leave to the national authorities the choice of form and methods.

A European regulation shall be a non-legislative act of general application for the implementation of legislative acts and of certain provisions of the Constitution. It may either be binding in its entirety and directly applicable in all Member States, or be binding, as to the result to be achieved, upon each Member State to which it is addressed, but shall leave to the national authorities the choice of form and methods.

A European decision shall be a non-legislative act, binding in its entirety. A decision which specifies those to whom it is addressed shall be binding only on them.

Recommendations and opinions shall have no binding force.

2. When considering draft legislative acts, the European Parliament and the Council shall refrain from adopting acts not provided for by the relevant legislative procedure in the area in question.

The distinction between legislative and non-legislative acts resides essentially in two elements of the Constitution that bring Union law closer to classical constitutional law. On the one hand, legislative acts are adopted by specific Institutions, namely, the European Parliament and the Council of Ministers, whereas non-legislative acts may be adopted by Institutions exercising an executive function. On the other hand, a legislative act takes precedence over a non-legislative act in a symbolic sense because, where the Institutions are permitted by the Constitution to choose between the two, the former is to be preferred. Analogies may be found in certain national legal orders, such as those in Germany (*Gesetzesvorbehalt*), Italy (*riserva della legge*) and Spain (*reserva de ley*), where there are so-called "hard core" areas of legislation that may not be delegated.

However, the Constitution does not take this logic so far as to establish an absolute hierarchy between laws and regulations by stipulating that the former necessarily trump the latter. To the contrary, the Constitution provides for a more complex system resembling the one invented in France in 1958 by the authors of the Constitution of the Fifth Republic, which distinguishes between those fields governed by laws and those governed by regulations (Articles 34 and 37 of the French Constitution). The hierarchy between laws and regulations was later fully embraced and re-established by the French *Conseil d'Etat* (i.e., the highest administrative court) and the French Constitutional Court through their jurisprudence. It cannot be ruled out that the Court of Justice will one day follow suit in respect of

European laws and regulations. Indeed, the introduction of a distinction between laws and regulations can further be seen in the reform of the legal bases for bringing legal action before the European Courts, as the procedures invoked to challenge a European law differ from those applying in the case of a European regulation (Article III-365 of the European Constitution).

Furthermore, the adoption of the concept of a European law is accompanied by a considerable strengthening of the European Parliament, which under the Constitution finally becomes a true co-legislator in respect of most fields in which the Union is competent to act. The Parliament has thus nearly reached the final stage of an evolution transforming its role from that of a mere consultative body, which it remained until the Single European Act of 1986, to that of a "co-decision" maker vested with veto rights in certain areas pursuant to the Treaty of Maastricht of 1992, and progressively to that of a true legislator by virtue of the Treaties of Amsterdam and of Nice in 1997 and 2000 respectively.

1.2.2. The Star-Crossed Legislative Council

The Convention's draft Constitution provided for a kind of separation of powers in relation to the composition and functions of the Council of Ministers. The difficulty faced by the Convention was to make it clear that the Council is responsible for two major activities that may be distinguished from each other. On the one hand, the Council functions as a lawmaker in areas of Union competence, while on the other hand it carries out the sort of policy orientation and decision-making activities that are more characteristic of a government.

The legislative function is shared by the Council of Ministers and the European Parliament, which together are charged with adopting European laws and framework laws (Articles 33 and III-302 of the Convention's text; Articles I-34 and III-396 of the final text). As far as the Council of Ministers is concerned, the Convention's text provided that its legislative functions were to be carried out by a specially designated configuration of the Council. As stipulated by Article 23 of the Convention's text (*Formations of the Council of Ministers*):

> When it acts in its legislative function, the Council of Ministers shall consider and, jointly with the European Parliament, enact European laws and European framework laws, in accordance with the provisions of the Constitution. In this function, each Member State's representation shall include one or two representatives at ministerial level with relevant expertise, reflecting the business on the agenda of the Council of Ministers.

Furthermore, Article 49 of the Convention's text (*Transparency of the proceedings of Union Institutions*) provided that the Council of Ministers, much like the Parliament, was to deliberate in public for the purposes of examining and adopting proposed legislation. Thus, a session of the *legislative* Council, consisting of

75 participants, would have been, according to the Convention's vision, a true democratic assembly. Yet the legislative Council did not live up to the hopes of certain members of the Convention. Some members had sought to radically separate the legislative Council from the General Affairs Council, in which the Ministers for European Affairs traditionally convene. Indeed, there were even proposals calling for the legislative Council to be composed of one Minister and two parliamentarians from each Member State. The opposition inspired by this proposal, whether or not justified by the peculiarities of the "Community method" (which implies the adoption by the Council and Parliament of legislative proposals by the Commission – see pages 21–24), confirm that this would have proved to be a significant innovation.

As it happened, the legislative Council was "the first victim" of the Foreign Ministers of the 25 Member States meeting in September of 2003 at Lake Garda in Italy to prepare the Intergovernmental Conference following the presentation of the Convention's draft Constitution to the European Council in June of that year. In relation to possible configurations of the Council of Ministers, Article I-24 of the final text of the Constitution refers only to the General Affairs Council and to the Foreign Affairs Council. Nevertheless, Article I-50 borrows from Article 49 of the Convention's text and provides that the Council must meet in public when considering and voting on legislative proposals. It is hoped that this provision will discourage Ministers, once back home in their capitals, from criticising European laws that they themselves have approved the day before in Brussels, a game played by politicians with some frequency.

1.2.3. The European Council President and the Union Minister
for Foreign Affairs

The creation of a permanent President of the Council (Article I-22 of the Constitution) and of a Minister of Foreign Affairs (Article I-28) are profound institutional innovations conceived by the Convention that have attracted the attention of numerous observers and commentators. The opinions expressed concerning these two new posts have been so diverse that, for anyone seeking to evaluate them objectively it is particularly difficult to identify their exact scope and implications.

From the terms of the Constitution it seems that the President of the Council is a position comparable to that of a head of State at the national level. However, as the stature of the President is not precisely defined, only through practice will it become clear whether this post will be akin to a Constitutional monarch who "reigns without governing", or to the Queen of England, or to a President of Italy (i.e., a moral authority and mediator between various political powers), or indeed to a French President of the Fifth Republic (an active arbitrator with a particularly strong role in foreign affairs). As for the Union Minister for Foreign Affairs, this post in fact succeeds the position of the EU's High Representative for the Common

Foreign and Security Policy (currently held by Javier Solana Madariaga, now in his second five-year term), which was established by the Treaty of Amsterdam in 1997. However, the Foreign Affairs Minister will differ from the High Representative in that he or she will also be a member of the Commission.

It is clear that the European Council has at last been formally inducted, in all material respects, into the Union as one of its principal Institutions. The provisions of the Constitution relating to the powers of the European Council are indeed more precise than those of any of the previous Treaties, which did not venture to define the European Council's nature or functions. The fact that the powers of the European Council are clearly delimited, and the fact that it now has a full-time President whose functions are incompatible with any national mandate, undeniably help to better define the separation of powers within the Union, both "horizontally" among the Institutions and "vertically" between the Union itself and the Member States.

On the other hand, the double allegiance of the Union Minister for Foreign Affairs highlights the fact that the responsibility for the elaboration and execution of the Common Foreign and Security Policy (CFSP) is shared by three of the Union's Institutions, namely, the European Council, the Commission, and the Council of Ministers. In addition, the final version of Article I-22, which sets forth the role and powers of the European Council President, is carefully worded so that it forbids the President from holding national office but it does not preclude the possibility that he or she might serve as a member of the European Parliament or of the Commission. Indeed, this approach is specifically intended to leave the door open to the possible future combination of the functions of the President of the Council and the President of the Commission.

Whenever the separation of powers is established in a constitution, regardless of whether the body politic is a parliamentary or presidential regime, such powers are most commonly divided among several institutions, as opposed to being held by just one. The European Constitution takes a further step in this direction, without however radically changing the pre-existing state of affairs. This comes as no surprise: although the Treaties of Rome and Maastricht are almost completely mute with respect to fundamental rights, the separation of powers has had a solid foundation at the supranational level ever since the creation of the European Coal and Steel Community (ECSC) in 1951.

1.3. The Weight of Words

The observations made thus far support the conclusion that the European Constitution is very much a part of the continuity created by its forerunners, the Treaties of Paris, Rome and Maastricht. The only real break with the past is an essentially formal one, although it is nevertheless significant. In particular, thanks to the Convention there is now only one integrated constitutional text, as opposed to an arcane series of treaties that have been propagating for more than 50 years.

The term *Constitution* – the root word for which is common to all romance languages, from English to Swedish (translated as *Verfassung* in German and *forvatning* in Danish but as *grondwet*, i.e., "fundamental law", in Dutch) – is generally associated with the concept of the State (rather than international organisations). This association is frequently taken for granted by a majority of politicians, jurists, social scientists and, above all, ordinary citizens. To call the text a *Constitution* is therefore far from an innocent gesture. And the adoption of the term (although a rather sterile academic debate lingers as to whether the text is a "Constitution" or a "Treaty") is one of the most extraordinary results of the European Convention.

1.3.1. The Treaties Establishing the European Communities and the Treaty on European Union

The Treaty of Paris of 18 April 1951 (which expired on 23 July 2002) was entitled the *Treaty establishing the European Coal and Steel Community* (ECSC), a motif that was reprised by the Treaties of Rome of 25 March 1957 *establishing* the European Economic Community (EEC) and *establishing* the European Community of Atomic Energy (commonly known as "Euratom"). Similarly, the Treaty of Paris of 27 May 1952 – ultimately aborted in 1954 – was called the Treaty *establishing* the European Defence Community (EDC). When the European Parliament on 14 February 1984 adopted a draft Treaty proposed by Altiero Spinelli, this document (which was never formally adopted by the Member States) was dubbed the Draft Treaty *establishing* the European Union.

The Treaty of Luxembourg and of The Hague of 17 and 28 February 1986, which signified the first major reform of the Treaties of Rome (i.e., the EC and Euratom Treaties) and hinted at a political community no longer merely economic in nature, was given an appellation that could hardly be more innocuous: "The Single European Act" (SEA). The name was chosen on the pretext that a single Treaty was being adopted to amend the earlier Treaties whereas, in reality, the SEA institutionalised political cooperation among the Member States (particularly in the area of foreign policy) outside the framework of those texts.

During the Intergovernmental Conference of 1991, certain national representatives, in particular those accompanying British Prime Minister John Major, insisted on avoiding the term *Treaty of Union*, which they claimed would risk giving the impression that a European State was being created. It may well be that the title had been reminiscent of the Treaty of 1707, which established the Union between England and Scotland. Since John Major also rejected the classic words "*Treaty establishing*", the Treaty instead took the inelegant name "Treaty *on* European Union", as if it were a collection of kitchen recipes.

1.3.2. The Breaking of a Taboo

Prior to the European Convention, any search for the word "Constitution" in the official texts relating to the European Communities and the European Union, or in the conclusions regularly produced by the Presidency of the European Council at the end of each summit (including the *Declaration on the future of the Union*, adopted at the Nice summit in December of 2000) was doomed to fail. In short, the word was noticeably absent from the EU's political vocabulary.

It was German Foreign Minister Joschka Fischer who finally broke the taboo against using the word "Constitution" in public. He did this on 12 May 2000 during a speech at Humboldt University in Berlin, in which he took up the proposition, advanced 50 years earlier by Robert Schuman, to work toward the realisation of a *fédération européenne*. In the months that followed, Fischer continued to invoke potent symbols: the arrival of the Euro in the pockets of EU citizens should be followed by the adoption of a European Constitution, much as the adoption of the Deutsche Mark in June of 1948 had been followed in May of 1949 by the promulgation of the *Grundgesetz* ("Basic Law") of the Federal Republic of Germany.

Although the term "Constitution" was in this case used to reflect the desire for meaningful progress toward a European federation, since Fischer's speech at Humboldt the word has no longer been reserved exclusively to the partisans of a more profound European integration. Indeed, the expression was soon thereafter also used by French President Jacques Chirac. This willingness to speak of a Constitution for Europe can be explained by the fact that, even avowed nationalists such as Charles Pasqua in France began to view the Constitution as a device capable of limiting the powers of the Institutions of the Union and of limiting its competences *vis-à-vis* those of the Member States.

At the Laeken summit in 2001, the European Council took the next bold step, without however allowing the issue to devolve into disorderly debate. The final Declaration adopted at Laeken in December of 2001 uses the formerly taboo word at the very end of a series of questions regarding the reorganisation and simplification of the contents of the Treaties.

Towards a *Constitution* for European citizens

[. . .]

The question ultimately arises as to whether this simplification and reorganisation might not lead in the long run to the adoption of a *constitutional text* in the Union. What might the basic features of such a constitution be? The values which the Union cherishes, the fundamental rights and obligations of its citizens, the relationship between Member States in the Union? (emphasis supplied)

The use of the term "Constitution" in discussing Europe's future did not have unanimous support. Indeed, even at the European Convention there was a long-standing preference for the more ambiguous expression "Constitutional Treaty". When Convention President Valéry Giscard d'Estaing presented the initial outline, or *squelette*, of the text, almost no one noticed that both the cover page used on 28 October 2002 and the press release of the next day bore the title "Treaty establishing a Constitution for Europe".

By the end of the Convention's proceedings in June of 2003, it seemed to be taken for granted that the Intergovernmental Conference (IGC) would use the term "Constitution", and the Convention's text was even published under the title "Constitution for Europe". Moreover, the version of 18 July 2003 underlined the importance of having symbols for the Union. Indeed, it contained a new provision specifically dedicated to such symbols (e.g., a flag, an anthem and a pan-European holiday) and, although the provision was in principle located in Part IV of the Convention's text (Article IV-1), it was nevertheless accompanied by a footnote stating that "[t]he Convention considers that this Article would be better situated in Part I". The IGC took the Convention's cue and decided to place the provision at the end of Title 1 of Part I of the Constitution, thus making it Article I-8 of the final text.

European Constitution, Article I-8

The symbols of the Union

The flag of the Union shall be a circle of twelve golden stars on a blue background.

The anthem of the Union shall be based on the "Ode to Joy" from the Ninth Symphony by Ludwig van Beethoven.

The motto of the Union shall be: "United in diversity".

The currency of the Union shall be the euro.

Europe day shall be celebrated on 9 May throughout the Union.

1.3.3. A Single, Clearer Text

Whatever impact symbols may have, the term *Constitution* only emerged and was only justified because the Convention decided, in the Autumn of 2002, after an initial "listening" phase, to respond affirmatively to the questions posed by the Laeken Declaration under the title "Towards a Constitution for European citizens" (see above). The vast majority of those stating their views in the sessions held during that initial phase – representatives of more or less structured interests, civil society and academics – had all declared their positive support for the "c" word.

Beyond the use of the term "Constitution", the most significant novelty in a formal sense, and the principal merit of the text adopted on 18 July 2003, was that it unified in a single text the Treaty establishing the European Community and the Treaty on European Union. This was undeniably done with a view toward making the substance of these texts more accessible to readers not specialised in Union law.

Why a "Constitution for Europe" and not a "Constitution of the European Union"? The question of what to call the text was posed by Convention President Valéry Giscard d'Estaing at the very beginning of the Convention's proceedings. Indeed, it had to be decided whether to restore the old name ("European Community"), or to maintain the existing one, or to trade in the current name for something else: *European Union, European Community, United Europe, United States of Europe*, and so on. A series of surveys were organised in various settings: the national press, groups that were more or less representative of civil society, etc. The majority of people polled indicated that they favoured maintaining the name "European Union".

Ironically, a certain number of supporters of reinforced European integration, who consider the Community method to be fundamental, found themselves side by side with eurosceptics in calling for a return to the name *European Community*. In a six-month period during the course of the proceedings in 2003, Convention member Jens-Peter Bonde from Denmark submitted hundreds of amendments, continuously substituting the word "Community" every time the word "Union" was used in the Praesidium's drafts.

2. What Hasn't Changed? A Constitution Without a State

2.1. Confederation versus Federation

The utility of a Constitution for Europe cannot be understood merely by analysing the changes that will be made to the law currently in force. Indeed, a comparison of the final text approved in June of 2004 and the Treaties of Rome and Maastricht indicates much more continuity than change, largely because a primary aim of the Constitution was to consolidate the principles to which the Union's fifteen Member States already adhered and to which the ten candidate countries, which acceded to the Union on 1 May 2004, had agreed to conform.

The European Constitution also defies explanation by simple reference to the national constitutions of pluralist democracies. Indeed, it bears many features which distinguish it substantially from such national constitutions and which contribute to the unique nature of the Union. In this regard, four essential points must be made.

The title of the Convention's text was the "Draft Treaty establishing a Constitution for Europe". The Convention thus remained faithful to the mandate with which it was charged, namely, to prepare proposals for the Intergovernmental Conference (IGC), the latter being the only organ with formal competence to reform the Treaties of Rome and Maastricht. Following the modifications of the IGC, the Convention's text has in fact become a "Constitution" – but a Constitution adopted by the common agreement of the Member States of the Union in the form of a Treaty and not a Constitution of a collection of individuals designed to create a State.

The Preamble of the United States Constitution of 1787 serves to illustrate the point made above, as it provides: "We the *People* of the United States [. . .] do ordain and establish this Constitution for the United States of America". (emphasis supplied) This is strikingly different from the Preamble of the European Constitution (see page 6 above), which was written in the name of the representatives of the Member States. In the case of the US, the delegates to the Constitutional Convention in Philadelphia, which convened to reform the Articles of Confederation of 1777 (i.e., the treaty binding the previously independent Thirteen Colonies together), proposed a Constitution in the sense of the constitution of a new *State*, in particular a State with a federal government.

Since that time, the view of legal scholars has been that the formal distinction between a *confederation* and a *federation* is that a *confederation* is based on a treaty between sovereign States, while a *federation* is based on a constitution adopted by a so-called *pouvoir constituant* ("constitutive power") most often consisting of the people but also occasionally of a monarch, as in the case of the *Constitutions octroyées* of the 19th Century (e.g., the *Statuto Albertino* in Italy in 1848 and the French Charters of 1814 and 1830).

The language of the European Constitution is written self-consciously to conform to a *constitutional* style as opposed to the style of the Treaties of Rome and Maastricht. Nevertheless, in terms of both form and content, the majority of the general and final provisions of Part IV of the Constitution (in particular, Articles IV-437 to IV-448) are written in a manner that underscores the continuity between the Constitution and its predecessors.

Beyond the symbolism of the Constitution, the nature of the document has significant legal consequences. To appreciate these, it is important to note first of all that the Treaties of Rome established a distinctive legal order for the Member States, which may be relied on by their citizens before both national courts and (if certain conditions are met) the European Courts in Luxembourg. Still, notwithstanding the uniqueness of this supranational legal order, the Treaties signed by the Member States – from the Treaties of Rome to the Treaty of Nice and indeed the Constitution itself – remain governed in the final analysis by public international law, or more precisely, by the norms and customs recognised and codified by the Vienna Convention on the Law of Treaties, signed in 1969.

Furthermore, despite a half-century of European integration, many of the constitutions of the Member States, and in particular those of the original six (i.e., France, Germany, Italy and the Benelux countries), either contain no reference to the Union whatsoever or make only the most indirect allusions to it. Consequently, in these countries the constitutional provisions relating to international treaties also apply to the various Treaties of the European Communities and the European Union (even if in some cases certain supplementary procedures are foreseen for their adoption), such as, for example, Article 23 of the German

Constitution following reforms made in 1992. Similarly, in Luxembourg – which has never hesitated to support the project of European integration – the national Constitution contains a single provision applicable to all international treaties. Article 49 *bis* of that Constitution, which was in fact introduced in view of European integration, provides that certain powers of the State may be delegated "by means of a treaty of institutions of international law", so long as such delegation is of a temporary nature.

2.2. A "European Union" and not a "United States of Europe"

Comparisons between the European Union and the United States are both inevitable and revealing, and it is no accident that the expression "United States of Europe" is no longer in vogue among the advocates of European integration in the way that it was in the times of Jean Monnet. The US is of course a sovereign State and a member of the international community. It is composed of subordinate states which, despite having their own institutions and state constitutions, are not endowed with the powers of a sovereign *State*. The relationships between the states in the US therefore have no connection, either in theory or in practice, with international relations. Furthermore, since the days of the US Civil War, the US has been more or less indivisible and, despite the wishes of certain radical factions in certain parts of the country, no state is allowed to secede.

By contrast, in the framework of the European Communities and the European Union, the Member States continue to maintain classic international relations: each one has diplomatic and consular representations in the other Member States, whose personnel enjoy the privileges and immunities recognised by the Vienna Conventions on Diplomatic Relations (1961) and Consular Relations (1963).

As for EU citizens residing in a Member State other than their own, while it is true that they benefit from many rights guaranteed to them by the Treaties (and in the future by the Constitution), they continue to be first and foremost citizens of their own Member State, which can intervene on their behalf by means of the classical mechanism of "diplomatic protection". Despite the greater privileges accorded to them compared with third country nationals, citizens of the Union residing in Member States other than their own are in fact governed by the same national legislation that applies to foreigners, subject to certain adjustments designed to ensure that, as between EU citizens, there is no discrimination. The European Constitution changes none of that.

The Constitution does, however, resolve an issue that had long been the subject of debate among legal scholars, namely, the question of secession. In this regard, the Constitution explicitly confirms the ability of a Member State to withdraw from the Union, and indeed establishes a corresponding set of procedures.

European Constitution, Article I-60

Voluntary withdrawal from the Union

1. Any Member State may decide to withdraw from the Union in accordance with its own constitutional requirements.

2. A Member State which decides to withdraw shall notify the European Council of its intention. In the light of the guidelines provided by the European Council, the Union shall negotiate and conclude an agreement with that State, setting out the arrangements for its withdrawal, taking account of the framework for its future relationship with the Union. That agreement shall be negotiated in accordance with Article III-325(3). It shall be concluded by the Council, acting by a qualified majority, after obtaining the consent of the European Parliament.

3. The Constitution shall cease to apply to the State in question from the date of entry into force of the withdrawal agreement or, failing that, two years after the notification referred to in paragraph 2, unless the European Council, in agreement with the Member State concerned, unanimously decides to extend this period.

4. For the purposes of paragraphs 2 and 3, the member of the European Council or of the Council representing the withdrawing Member State shall not participate in the discussions of the European Council or Council or in European decisions concerning it.

A qualified majority shall be defined as at least 72% of the members of the Council, representing the participating Member States, comprising at least 65% of the population of these States.

5. If a State which has withdrawn from the Union asks to rejoin, its request shall be subject to the procedure referred to in Article I-58 [*Conditions of eligibility and procedure for accession to the Union*].

2.3. The "Community Method"

Once the European Constitution enters into force, the European *Community* will cease to exist, as it will merge with and effectively be subsumed by the Union. However, perhaps counter-intuitively, it is clear from Article 1 of the Constitution that the Union will continue to have at its disposal the *Community method* (described below), which indeed will constitute the most important means of promulgating Union legislation.

The tenor of Article 1 was clear from the very first plenary sessions in which the members of the Convention began debating the draft Constitution. President Giscard d'Estaing insisted repeatedly on two points. Firstly, the Union would continue (as has been provided for since the Treaty of Maastricht) to coordinate national policies in those fields in which it has not been attributed competence by the Member States, that is to say, essentially, in the fields of the Common Foreign and Security Policy (CFSP) and defence. Secondly, and consistent with the Treaties of Paris and Rome, the Union would exercise competences attributed "on a federal basis", that is, by the three main common Institutions: the Parliament, the Commission and the Council of Ministers.

European Constitution, Article I-1

Establishment of the Union

1. Reflecting the will of the citizens and the States of Europe to build a common future, this Constitution establishes the European Union, on which the Member States confer competences to attain objectives they have in common. The Union shall coordinate the policies by which the Member States aim to achieve these objectives, and shall exercise on a Community basis the competences they confer on it.

2. The Union shall be open to all European States which respect its values and are committed to promoting them together.

However, attempts to introduce the word *federal* into the Treaties have consistently run up against the frank opposition of the British government. For example, in 1991, British Prime Minister John Major rejected a proposal advanced by German Chancellor Helmut Kohl and French President François Mitterand to incorporate the term *vocation fédérale* in the Treaty of Maastricht, as such an expression would have implied, in his view, an evolution of the Union in the direction of some form of State. Although the *on a federal basis* formula discussed in the Convention in 2002 was in itself a compromise with respect to the earlier proposal of Kohl and Mitterand, this formula remained unsatisfactory for the British delegation. Following a visit with British Prime Minister Tony Blair, Giscard was persuaded that it would be necessary to strike the word "federal" from the text and refer instead to a Union exercising competences "on a *Community* basis".

To the extent that resistance to the word "federal" reflects an underlying desire to limit the process of European integration, the British government's success in imposing more restrained language seems little more than a Pyrrhic victory. Indeed, while no one really knows what significance the term *federal* might have in the context of European integration, the Community method has been clearly defined ever since it was invented by Jean Monnet and his collaborators when the Schuman plan was conceived in 1950. This unique form of policy-making is based on two essential elements: the powers of the Commission; and the so-called "functionalist" approach to European integration.

2.3.1. The Powers of the Commission

The European Commission is an innovative institution that has no model or equivalent, either in national constitutions or in international organisations. It is, in principle, an independent organ charged with promoting the general European interest (as opposed to the interests of the Member States as such) through the exercise of three functions in particular that had traditionally been executed only by States:

- First, the Commission plays a decisive role in the promulgation of Union legislation, as it is entrusted with an exclusive "right of initiative", i.e., the exclusive right to propose such legislation, subject to certain rare exceptions;

- Second, the Commission is the Union's principal executive organ, as it is responsible for the direct application of various common policies, including, e.g., competition policy (an area in which it has wide powers to adopt binding decisions), budget management (particularly in respect of the Union's Common Agricultural Policy), structural funds (i.e., funds aimed at the economic development of disadvantaged regions), research policy, and development aid;
- Third, the Commission has certain quasi-judicial powers, reminiscent of those of a public prosecutor, as it may bring proceedings before the European Court of Justice against Member States in breach of their legal obligations (whether stemming directly from the Treaties or where otherwise imposed by Union legislation).

The Commission and the services it provides are certainly not above reproach, and they often inspire the same kinds of criticisms generally directed toward national governments and administrations. Nevertheless, it is clear that the attribution to the Commission of the legislative, executive and "prosecutorial" powers described above has assured the capacity of the Community method to drive forward the process of integration in cases where the more classical means of intergovernmental cooperation have proved unable to do so.

Among the powers of the Commission, the general public is probably least familiar with those of a prosecutorial nature. However, the Commission's role of enforcer is the most crucial of all. Indeed, experience has shown that the Member States cannot be counted on to bring enforcement actions against each other: as each one has at least a few skeletons in its closet, as it were, such an action would run the risk of setting off a cycle of mutual reprisals. As for private enforcement actions, these can be very effective in particular cases, but such actions are risky and they certainly do not suffice, on the whole, to impress a recalcitrant government.

The Constitution maintains intact the Commission's powers as well as the unique scheme of separation of powers which they serve to guarantee. Consequently, by virtue of its exclusive right of initiative (other than in certain policy fields that have always fallen outside the Commission's competence), the Commission will retain its ability to determine which legislative proposals are advanced and thus to filter out laws and regulations tainted by excessive intergovernmental horse-trading or otherwise contrary to the general European interest.

Many specialists consider, with good reason, that certain policies executed by the Commission are ill-conceived, or no longer appropriate under current conditions, or poorly managed. However, the Constitution does not provide any guidance concerning policy management, and this is understandable since that is not really the role of a Constitution. Instead, consistent with the Treaty of Rome, the Constitution only sets forth the fields in which the Institutions of the Union are competent and by which procedures the Institutions may act. It does not dictate what the Union's policies will actually be, let alone how such policies are to be applied.

2.3.2. *The "Functionalist" Approach*

Since the Schuman Declaration of 9 May 1950, the process of European integration has also been associated with what is sometimes called a "functionalist" approach. The terms *functionalist* and, more recently, *neo-functionalist*, which are primarily found in the works of political scientists, denote a theoretical construct used to apply the practical method devised by Jean Monnet that is now commonly known as the Community method. Monnet's ideas had been inspired on the one hand by his experience in sophisticated logistics operations linking France, the UK and the United States during World Wars I and II and, on the other hand, by his subsequent involvement in the development and application of the Marshall Plan for the reconstruction of Europe. The *functionalist* approach may be recognised in a famous passage from the Schuman Declaration (which in fact had been written by Monnet and his assistants): "Europe will not be made all at once, or according to a single plan. It will be built through concrete achievements which first create a *de facto* solidarity." From these words it may be inferred that European integration is a process of accretion whereby the interests of different States become, above all for pragmatic reasons, increasingly intertwined.

The academic literature on European integration continues to this day to debate the nature, limits, virtues and defects of this pragmatic approach. However, the oft-neglected essential point is that the Community method is a distinctively *supple* mechanism. It is unconstrained by a rigid definition of the powers to be exercised in common, and it has a flexible institutional design that has allowed for, most notably, the progressive reinforcement of the role of the European Parliament.

When the European Convention opened its proceedings, there was substantial pressure to rein in all of this flexibility and establish more clearly delineated boundaries. Such pressure was applied not only by those hostile to integration, but also by institutions such as the German *Länder*, which blamed the Union for what they perceived to be a loss of their power and influence, and by experts of diverse interests, who noted the ineffectiveness of certain Community policies.

In the end, however, the Convention managed to resist this pressure. The flexibility and openness that are fundamental to the functionalist approach is in fact reflected in Article I-3 of the Constitution (which defines the Union's objectives), read in conjunction with Article I-18. This latter provision is commonly called the "flexibility clause" because it confirms that the Union has implied powers of action, analogous in some respects to the "Necessary and Proper" Clause in the US Constitution, but of much more limited scope in that it can only be invoked on the basis of unanimity in the Council of Ministers. Article I-18 is yet another mark of continuity with the Treaty of Rome, and borrows from it the essential substance of Article 308 (ex-Article 235) while refining it and adapting the corresponding procedure to take account of the enhanced powers of the European Parliament.

European Constitution

Article I-3: The Union's Objectives	Article I-18: Flexibility Clause
1.The Union's aim is to promote peace, its values and the well-being of its peoples.	1. If action by the Union should prove necessary within the framework of the policies defined in Part III, to attain one of the objectives set out in the Constitution, and the Constitution has not provided the necessary powers, the Council of Ministers, acting unanimously on a proposal from the European Commission and after obtaining the consent of the European Parliament, shall adopt the appropriate measures.
2. The Union shall offer its citizens an area of freedom, security and justice without internal frontiers, and an internal market where competition is free and undistorted.	2. Using the procedure for monitoring the subsidiarity principle referred to in Article I-11(3), the European Commission shall draw national Parliaments' attention to proposals based on this Article.
3. The Union shall work for the sustainable development of Europe based on balanced economic growth and price stability, a highly competitive social market economy, aiming at full employment and social progress, and a high level of protection and improvement of the quality of the environment. It shall promote scientific and technological advance.	3. Measures based on this Article shall not entail harmonisation of Member States' laws or regulations in cases where the Constitution excludes such harmonisation.
It shall combat social exclusion and discrimination, and shall promote social justice and protection, equality between women and men, solidarity between generations and protection of the rights of the child.	
It shall promote economic, social and territorial cohesion, and solidarity among Member States.	
It shall respect its rich cultural and linguistic diversity, and shall ensure that Europe's cultural heritage is safeguarded and enhanced.	
4. In its relations with the wider world, the Union shall uphold and promote its values and interests. It shall contribute to peace, security, the sustainable development of the Earth, solidarity and mutual respect among peoples, free and fair trade, eradication of poverty and the protection of human rights, in particular the rights of the child, as well as to the strict observance and the development of international law, including respect for the principles of the United Nations Charter.	
5. The Union shall pursue its objectives by appropriate means commensurate with the competences which are conferred upon it in the Constitution.	

25

2.4. The "European Economic Constitution"

From the time it was adopted in 1957, the Treaty of Rome had one conspicuous element that distinguished it from the constitutions of the Member States (although it is true that the texts adopted by France in 1946, by Italy in 1947 and by Germany in 1949 all endeavoured to enshrine the economic and social objectives marking the post-war period in Western Europe). In particular, the Treaty fixed, in legal terms, the principles and rules governing the functioning of a market economy in which there is: free interplay between supply and demand; freedom of movement of goods, services, workers and capital across national frontiers; and a clear set of competition rules. The virtues of the market were exalted for two reasons. Firstly, the authors of the Treaty were convinced that an open market economy was the most effective mechanism (or at least that it was the least defective) to achieve prosperity. Secondly, they believed that powerful cartels, in the absence of a solid set of competition rules, had contributed to the success of the dictators in Europe, and above all to the rearmament of Germany, and hence to the horrors of war.

The primary aim of the Treaty was thus to give life to a market economy on a European scale through the exaltation of the "four freedoms" (i.e., freedom of cross-border movement of goods, services, workers and capital) and of the competition rules, while at the same time leaving the Member States free to make their own choices in matters of social welfare. For example, the prerogatives of the Member States regarding property rights were explicitly guaranteed by Article 295 (ex-Article 222) of the Treaty of Rome, which states that "[t]his Treaty shall in no way prejudice the rules in Member States governing the system of property ownership". This provision is now reproduced in Article III-425 of the Constitution.

The economic situation in Europe, and the prevailing conceptions relating to the nature of the Welfare State, have of course changed considerably over the last 50 years. And there is evidence of evolving points of emphasis in the Constitution compared to its forerunners. Indeed, within the text one may discern an attempt to balance and synthesise: the *acquis* of the Treaty of Rome (i.e., the ensemble of its rules and principles); the European-style conception of a "*social* market economy", which emphasises social "solidarity"; and the sensitive traditions and anxieties associated with certain Member States.

Three provisions of the Constitution in particular are intended to achieve such a synthesis. Firstly, the text of Article I-3 (which, as explained above, sets forth the objectives of the Union – and which was redrafted many times) reaffirms several essential points:

1. The Union shall offer its citizens [. . .] an *internal market* where *competition* is free and undistorted.

2. The Union shall work for the *sustainable development* of Europe based on *balanced economic growth* and price stability, a *highly competitive social market economy*, aiming at *full employment* and *social progress* [. . .].

It shall promote *economic, social and territorial cohesion*, and *solidarity* among Member States. (emphasis supplied)

Secondly, Article I-4 of the Constitution, entitled *Fundamental freedoms and non-discrimination*, enshrines the foundations of the European Economic Community as established by the Treaty of Rome:

1. The free movement of persons, services, goods and capital, and freedom of establishment shall be guaranteed within and by the Union, in accordance with the Constitution.
2. Within the scope of the Constitution, and without prejudice to any of its specific provisions, any discrimination on grounds of nationality shall be prohibited.

Finally, the Charter of Fundamental Rights of the Union in Part II of the Constitution proclaims certain social rights in Articles II-74 to II-76 and Articles II-87 to II-98. These rights should in time lead to a balance between the Constitution's market-oriented rules and the objectives of solidarity in the Union's legislation and policies. On the one hand, the social rights may serve to attenuate any simplistic application of the principles of competition developed in the case law of the European Courts. On the other hand, they may help to preserve the particularities of the various national social welfare systems, provided they do not create distortions of a discriminatory nature among the Member States.

It is worth noting finally that the Intergovernmental Conference added a new social provision of general scope in Part III of the Constitution (which covers the policies and functioning of the Union). According to this provision (Article III-117), the Union must take into account "requirements linked to the promotion of a high level of employment, the guarantee of adequate social protection, the fight against social exclusion, and a high level of education, training and protection of human health". This provision confirms the continuing evolution of the "Constitution" of the Union from one based strictly on economic concerns to one that has both economic and social underpinnings.

3. IMPARFAITE MAIS INESPÉRÉE

It is only too easy to lapse into ironising on the way the Constitution was drafted. Given the considerable number of provisions reprised from the previously existing Treaties without any significant modifications, some observers will undoubtedly ask: *What was the point of 18 months of work by the Convention, followed by 10 months of negotiations among the Member States?* Meanwhile, specialists in Community law with a conservative bent may well complain about the new provisions (not to mention the fact that they will have to learn another new set of numbers, without forgetting the old ones). Those in the federalist camp will surely regret the missed opportunity to move further down the road to integration. Finally, sceptics will take delight in ridiculing the gushing lyricism of the Preamble and of many new provisions.

Be that as it may, the Constitution will serve to consolidate, clarify and create a better structure for the Union and its activities. The first comment of Valéry Giscard d'Estaing, and of those who were able to closely follow the proceedings of the Convention, was: *"imparfaite mais inespérée"* ("imperfect, but beyond what could be hoped for"). And in this context the word *inespérée* should not be underestimated! Indeed, the risk of failure loomed over the Convention until the very end. The diversity of the Convention's members, divided as they were by national and political cleavages as well as by divergent views of Europe's future, did not make the task an easy one. And the growing pressures applied by national governments, as they realised little by little that something significant was transpiring, threatened on several occasions to derail the process. The failure to reach a unanimous accord among the 25 participating countries during the Italian Presidency in December of 2003 aroused fears that the Constitution might be killed at birth. But then, optimism sprang up, due in particular to deft diplomatic efforts by the Irish Presidency (and perhaps also due in some measure to a change of government in Spain) in the months leading up to the Brussels summit of June 2004. Furthermore, many observers feared throughout the IGC that tampering by the Member States would disfigure the text, possibly beyond recognition. However, in the end the Constitution was spared this fate, as the most essential innovations introduced by the Convention survived the IGC.

Now that the Constitution is in its final form and is traversing the bumpy road of ratification, an avalanche of critical commentary may be expected. Some commentators will present a fair and balanced perspective; for others this may not be of the slightest concern. In any event, to carry out an *objective* evaluation of the Constitution, it is necessary to proceed according to a three-part exercise:

– Firstly, the final text must be compared not only with the texts of the pre-existing Treaties but also with the interpretations of those texts that have been adopted by the Union's Institutions and the operational consequences of such interpretations;
– Secondly, the Convention process must be both *understood* – for example in terms of its composition, procedures and internal dynamics, as well as the wider context in which it was working (including in particular the crisis produced by the war in Iraq) – and *compared* with the laborious negotiations of the IGC that followed it; and
– Thirdly, an attempt must be made to read the stars and divine how the text might potentially develop and affect the Union's citizens, Member States and Institutions.

THE EUROPEAN CONSTITUTION:
WHAT IS IT, EXACTLY?

"*È un maschio!*", exclaimed Giuliano Amato (former Prime Minister of Italy and Vice-President of the Convention), referring to the text which the Convention had just ushered into the world in June of 2003: "It's a boy!" And this remark plays on the fact that, in Italian, the word for "treaty" (*tratatto*) is masculine, whereas Amato would have preferred a "girl", since the word *Costituzione* is feminine. The remark was thus a kind of gentle indictment of the Convention for its lack of boldness, i.e., for its failure to go beyond the existing Treaties and transform them into a true Constitution. Amato also made reference to Neil Jordan's film *The Crying Game*, in which a militant of the IRA holding a British soldier captive falls in love with his prisoner's girlfriend, only to find in due course that this "girlfriend" is in fact a transvestite.

The point Vice-President Amato was making related above all to the heavy procedure for making future amendments to the Constitution, which will remain the exclusive province of the Member States, in the style of a Treaty, and which therefore has not been entrusted to the Union's Institutions as might be more in keeping with a classical constitution. However, despite his disappointment with the sex of the child, Amato noted that the Convention's text also had certain feminine genes that could perhaps in the future allow it to blossom and realise its constitutional potential.

Of course, the Constitution is bound to provoke a variety of sentiments, depending on one's point of view. For example, Giscard's three-word assessment – "*imparfaite mais inespérée*" – may remind film buffs of the final moments of Billy Wilder's film *Some Like it Hot*. When Jack Lemmon admits to Joe E. Brown that he is in reality a man, Brown replies: "Nobody's perfect!"

In any event, it is clear that the imperfect but impressive text produced by the Convention – later adopted mostly intact by the European Council – is a *hybrid* text reflecting hard-won compromises between opposing visions of the purpose and direction of European integration. Observers attentive to the composition and the functioning of the Convention will note that, although its members might be grouped into a number of political parties and although they quite naturally represented their various national and institutional interests, from a broader perspective they reflected four distinct visions of Europe's future, as will be further explained in the next chapter.

1. A TREATY LAYING THE FOUNDATIONS OF A CONSTITUTION

1.1. A Complete Draft and not just a Catalogue of Options

In point of fact, the Convention was not given a mandate to draft a Constitution, whether in the form of a Treaty or otherwise. The Convention was thus not in the position of, for example, the government of General de Gaulle, obliged by the law of 3 June 1958 to prepare a draft constitutional law for France, or the group of experts who met in August of 1948 at a Bavarian castle in Herrenchiemsee to draw up a draft *Grundgesetz* for the *Länder* occupied by the allied forces. By contrast, the Convention was merely charged with presenting a "final document", essentially setting forth reflections and propositions, which was to be a "starting point" and which was to have no more legal value than any synthesis of the national debates concerning the future of Europe that this "final document" was expected to provoke.

Laeken Declaration of 15 December 2001 (excerpt)

Final Document

The Convention will consider the various issues. It will draw up a final document which may comprise either different options, indicating the degree of support which they received, or recommendations if consensus is achieved. Together with the outcome of national debates on the future of the Union, the final document will provide a starting point for discussions in the Intergovernmental Conference, which will take the ultimate decisions.

This is not to suggest that the preparation of a complete text was not contemplated by some. To the contrary, a more ambitious project was envisaged by certain delegations of the European Council and certainly by the candidates being considered for the Convention Presidency. However, in December of 2001 a unanimous agreement to take such a bold step was politically impossible. Therefore, in light of its origins and background, it is rather unfair to fault the Convention for not showing more audacity than it did. No one will know for sure what was the optimal balance between audacity and realism until the various parliaments and populations of the Member States have entered their verdict on the text approved by the European Council in June of 2004. Another point must also be made: if the Convention's text had had a title such as "Draft Constitution" instead of the longer and more technically accurate "Draft Treaty establishing a Constitution for Europe", it might well have suffered the same fate as countless other drafts and reports, tucked away in a drawer and consigned to oblivion.

The Presidency and the Secretariat of the Convention both took the greatest care to avoid falling into the trap of devising "options" for the Union, and to deliver instead a complete draft text to the European Council. This can be understood in part by recalling the events leading up to the Treaty of Amsterdam. In 1996-97, in anticipation of the IGC that was scheduled to meet and to adopt that Treaty, a "reflection group", led by Spanish Minister of European Affairs Carlos Westendorp, was charged with preparing the IGC's work. Westendorp's group sought to clear the debate-filled air by presenting majority and minority opinions on every issue without indicating which states held which positions. However, this approach proved fruitless: when the IGC convened in Amsterdam, the report concerning these majority and minority positions – rather than facilitating the negotiations – inadvertently contributed to a hardening of the Member States' views.

This lesson was not lost on the key members of the Convention, who presented the European Council with a comprehensive, ready-made text in Thessaloniki in June 2003. The great hope was that the text would not fall victim to the political vagaries of the IGC, which had the prerogative to unravel the document, rearrange it and adjust it until it had lost all of its design, symmetry and cohesion.

The contents of the Convention's text corresponded, as suggested in Chapter 1, to those of a Constitution in the tradition of the Enlightenment. Despite the retention of the extraordinarily difficult amendment procedure, and despite the medium-sized backward steps taken by the IGC (which could hardly be compensated for by its tiny steps forward), the final text as adopted in fact undeniably bears the marks of an incipient but real Constitution, in terms of both its symbolic provisions and the procedures it sets forth.

1.2. More than just another Treaty between States

The symbolic aspects of Constitutions have always been one of their most important features. Sceptics might say that the use of symbols is merely a kind of lip service and that such symbols are normally mute declarations of no concrete relevance. However, lawyers know that symbols can be much more than they seem and can have a significant impact on how texts are interpreted by courts and other political institutions. For that matter, a constitution is itself a highly potent symbol that can affect the way a society functions in important ways.

Those members of the Convention that pushed hardest for the Constitution's symbolic provisions were firmly convinced that these provisions would contribute to the future durability of the European edifice. Lawyers, in particular, are well aware of the fact that, in a constitutional text, a seemingly innocent or purely declaratory citation may be transformed into potent weapons in the hands of citizens and interest groups when appearing before courts, parliamentary commissions and administrative offices. The Constitution's provisions regarding the rights of citizens of the Union (in particular, Articles I-1 and I-46 and the whole of Part II) and those recognising local democracy (Articles III-386 to III-388) provide two clear examples.

With respect to the first example, it will be recalled that the Treaty of Maastricht of 1992 created the notion of a "European citizenship" to make transparent a number of political rights which Union law bestows upon the citizens of the Member States. In the draft of 2003 the Convention strove to enhance the visibility of such rights (without creating new ones). This can clearly be seen from Article 1, first sentence, of the Convention's text:

> Reflecting the will of the citizens and States of Europe to build a common future, this Constitution establishes the European Union, on which the Member States confer competences to attain objectives they have in common.

It may seem as if this sentence merely states the obvious. However, the wording of the sentence inspired heated debates and indeed attracted numerous proposed amendments by the members of the Convention. And the controversy surrounding the way the sentence is phrased may be explained by its symbolic significance. In the end, notwithstanding the ardent efforts of some who favoured a different formulation, the equivalent provision in the Constitution, Article I-1, puts the citizens of the Union before the Member States. This symbolic, inaugural Article of the Constitution is reinforced by two groundbreaking elements that do not appear in the existing Treaties: the incorporation of the Charter of Fundamental Rights in Part II of the Constitution and the insertion, in Part I, of a Title (Title VI) devoted to the *democratic life* of the Union, of which Article I-46 in particular stresses the importance of the Union's citizens. The principle of equality of the Union's citizens before the Constitution is picked up by Article I-45, which contains the unaltered text of Article 44 of the Convention's text.

European Constitution

Part I, Title VI: The Democratic Life of the Union	Article I-46: The Principle of Representative Democracy
Article I-45: the principle of democratic equality	1. The functioning of the Union shall be founded on representative democracy.
Article I-46: the principle of representative democracy (see second column)	2. Citizens are directly represented at Union level in the European Parliament.
Article I-47: the principle of participatory democracy	Member States are represented in the European Council by their Heads of State or Government and in the Council by their governments, themselves democratically accountable either to their national Parliaments, or to their citizens.
Article I-48: the social partners and autonomous social dialogue	
Article I-50: transparency of the proceedings of the Union institutions, bodies, offices and agencies	

European Constitution (Cont'd)

Part I, Title VI: The Democratic Life of the Union	Article I-46: The Principle of Representative Democracy
Article I-51: protection of personal data Article I-52: status of churches and non-confessional organisations	3. Every citizen shall have the right o participate in the democratic life of the Union. Decisions shall be taken as openly and as closely as possible to the citizen. 4. Political parties at European level contribute to forming European political awareness and to expressing the will of citizens of the Union.

Turning to the second example mentioned above relating to the recognition of democracy at the local level, it is important to consider that international treaties generally do not take account of municipalities, provinces, regions or other sub-national units. Such entities are simply regarded as being parts of the contracting State, and it is normally taken for granted that the State represents their interests. The European Charter of Local Self-Government, adopted by the Council of Europe (to which all of the EU's Member States belong) in 1985, is a notable exception to this general rule.

Indeed, the normal tendency at the international level to pay little heed to local and regional units applies even with respect to federal States. To put this in perspective, the two most prominent systems of constitutional federalism should be considered. First, there is the American system, which is a Union of non-sovereign states. In this system, matters concerning *sub*-state authorities (in particular, cities and counties) fall within the states' exclusive competence (although the competences and interests of cities and counties may nevertheless be the subject of federal legislation). Sub-state authorities are not protected by the Tenth Amendment of the federal Constitution, according to which powers not delegated to the federal government are reserved to the States or to the people. The second most prominent federalist system is found in Germany. In some respects the German system is similar to that of the United States, i.e., it is a Union of "states", called *Länder*, who have exclusive competence in respect of the organisation and functioning of localities. At the same time, however, German constitutional law recognises the principle of local autonomy (*Grundsatz der Kommunalen Selbstverwaltung*), which may be invoked if necessary before relevant jurisdictions and, in particular, before the Federal Constitutional Court.

The Constitution incorporates an obligation on the Union that reflects a shift away from the American tradition in favour of the German constitutional model. The combined efforts of certain Convention members, led by Jean-Luc Dehaene and by the delegates of the Committee of the Regions (one of the Union's advisory bodies, governed by Articles III-386 to III-388 of the Constitution and dedicated to regional interests), led to a plenary session of the Convention on 7 February 2003 concerning the role of regional and local authorities in Europe. The fruits of that session can be seen in Article 5(1) of the Convention's text, entitled *Relations between the Union and the Member States*, which provides that:

> The Union shall respect the national identities of the Member States, inherent in their fundamental structures, political and constitutional, *inclusive of regional and local self-government.* (emphasis supplied)

The initial versions of Article 5(1) even made reference to public authorities at the regional and local levels, much like the Preamble to the Charter of Fundamental Rights. The Italian and German versions of Article 5(1) are of particular interest in that they adopt the formulations used in national constitutional law for the protection of self-government. In Italian, the expression is: "*compreso il sistema delle autonomie regionali e locali*", while in German the same idea is conveyed by "*einschließlich der regionalen und kommunalen Selbstverwaltung*". In addition, the role of regional and local units must also be recognised, especially those regions with legislative powers. These entities are specifically referred to in the Protocol on the application of the principles of subsidiarity and proportionality (originally adopted as part of the Treaty of Amsterdam).

Article 5 appeared in the Convention's text as one of only eight Articles contained in Title I (*Definition and objectives of the Union*). Its prominent place confirms that regions and localities form an integral part of the complex system of the Union. The formulation adopted by the Convention shrewdly avoids interfering in the internal affairs of the Member States, as it evokes the regional and local dimensions only as concerns the respect by the Union for the national identity of the Member States. No right of action is created in favour of sub-national units as against their own Member States, as in the German Constitution. Yet the text of Article 5 goes beyond that of the Tenth Amendment of the US Constitution, which ignores cities and counties despite the fact that in the American system local democracy plays a fundamental role.

The Intergovernmental Conference, under the Irish Presidency, added a reference to the principle of the equality of the Member States but otherwise maintained the Convention's wording in its entirety. In its final form, Article I-5 thus states:

> The Union shall respect the equality of Member States before the Constitution as well as their national identities, inherent in their fundamental structures, political and constitutional, inclusive of regional and local self-government.

1.3. Paving the Way for a True Constitution

When contemplating the procedure traditionally used for adopting amendments, a majority of the Convention's *Praesidium* (i.e., the Giscard-led group of 12 primarily responsible for preparing drafts) declined to redesign it and to create a system purely internal to the Union. In the United States, Article V of the federal Constitution establishes (in addition to an as-yet untried mechanism whereby the states may call for a Constitutional Convention) that amendments must first be approved by a two-thirds majority in both the House of Representatives and the Senate and must then be ratified by three-fourths of the states. The period of time necessary to fulfil these procedural criteria can occasionally call for extraordinary patience: the last modification made to the Constitution was the Twenty-Seventh Amendment, which entered into force in 1992 following ratification by the state of Michigan. The text of this amendment had in fact been adopted by Congress on the proposal of James Madison in 1789, together with the original Bill of Rights! The wheels of constitutional change can thus revolve at an excruciatingly slow pace, as the required three-fourths majority of the states (currently 38 states) is sometimes an elusive threshold.

This example of a revision to the US Constitution indicates that what matters is not so much the duration of the procedure but rather the respective powers of the Union and of the states. The mechanisms used around the world for the purpose of adopting constitutional amendments are so diverse, and cover such a wide gamut from the most flexible to the most rigid, that it would be a mistake to assess the true character of the European Union according to the rigidity of the amendment procedure. It would likewise be mistaken to suppose that a procedure somewhat lighter than the unanimous vote normally required by the European Constitution would be any guarantee of smoother and swifter evolution, as the example of the Americans' Twenty-Seventh Amendment serves to demonstrate. The issue of revising the European Constitution is thus an important question of principle. Should amendments be made by government representatives functioning "outside" the Constitution? Or should an institution *established by* the Constitution modify it from the inside? Treaties are amended from the outside; constitutions are amended from within.

Although the Convention's text maintained the ordinary revision procedure set forth in the Treaty of Maastricht (and inherited from the Treaty of Rome), a new provision was added allowing for a consultation of the Convention in important cases. This new procedure appears in Article IV-7(2) of the Convention's text and Article IV-443(2) of the final Constitution:

If the European Council, after consulting the European Parliament and the Commission, adopts by a simple majority a decision in favour of examining the proposed amendments, the President of the European Council shall convene a Convention composed of representatives of the national Parliaments, of the Heads of State or Government of the Member States, of the European Parliament and of the Commission. The European Central Bank shall also be consulted in the case of institutional changes in the monetary area. The Convention shall examine the proposals for amendments and shall adopt by consensus a recommendation to a conference of representatives of the governments of the Member States as provided for in paragraph 3.

The European Council may decide by a simple majority, after obtaining the consent of the European Parliament, not to convene a Convention should this not be justified by the extent of the proposed amendments. In the latter case, the European Council shall define the terms of reference for a conference of representatives of governments of the Member States.

The Constitution also provides other possible avenues for adopting amendments. Although the IGC, in Article IV-444 (*Simplified revision procedure*), made it more difficult to invoke the so-called *passerelle* clause (or "bridging clause") which had appeared in Article 24 of the Convention's text, it introduced a new simplified procedure which the Convention dared not add, for amending the provisions contained in Title III of Part III (i.e., those concerning internal Union policies and action). The ordinary revision procedure, the scaled-back *passerelle* clause, and the new simplified procedure (Article IV-445), are all presented in the table at page 37.

The *passerelle* clause is not entirely novel. For example, such a provision could already be found in Article K9 of the Treaty of Maastricht, which permitted the transfer of certain competences from the Union to the Community. This has made it possible to consign certain matters in the realm of Justice and Home Affairs – traditionally part of the Union's third pillar and hence subject to intergovernmental decision-making – to the first pillar, where the Community method applies. The Treaty of Amsterdam also contained analogous provisions. However, the most important of the *passerelles* was Article 138 of the Treaty of Rome, which empowered the Council, acting on unanimity, to decide that Members of the European Parliament could be elected by direct, universal suffrage. This important step toward democracy was in fact taken in December of 1974, at the initiative of Valéry Giscard d'Estaing in his earlier incarnation as the President of France.

The innovative feature of the *passerelle* that had been proposed by the Convention was its generality. The Convention's *passerelle* had important implications for the division of powers between the Union and the Member States, as it would have enabled the European Council to shift voting requirements in sensitive areas from unanimity – which permits each Member State to block a measure without having to justify its veto – to qualified majority, which obliges States opposing a measure to find allies.

The *simplified revision procedure* contained in Article IV-444 of the Constitution embraces the Convention's *passerelle* but makes it more rigid. According to Article IV-444, where Part III requires the Council of Ministers to act by unanimity in a given area or case (except where there are military implications), the European Council may unanimously adopt a European decision authorising the Council of Ministers to act by qualified majority. In addition, where Part III provides that European laws or frameworks laws must be adopted according to a *special* legislative procedure (i.e., an unusually stringent procedure short of unanimity), the European Council may unanimously adopt a European decision to the effect that the *ordinary* legislative procedure may be used instead. However, whereas Article 24 of the Convention's text would have allowed the European Council to change procedures by taking a unanimous decision after merely consulting the European Parliament and notifying the national parliaments, Article IV-444 requires not only unanimity on the part of the European Council but also the affirmative consent of the European Parliament and furthermore allows any national parliament to veto the initiative.

On the other hand, if a national parliament wishes to block the measure, it must do so within six months or else waive its rights. Moreover, unlike Article IV-445 (i.e., the new simplified revision procedure pertaining to internal Union policies and action), Article IV-444 does not require ratification by the Member States in accordance with their respective constitutional requirements. The risk of blockages that might otherwise result from, in particular, the opposition of national parliaments, proceedings of national Constitutional Courts, or national referendums is thus avoided because it is *at the moment the Constitution is ratified* that the availability of the *passerelle* will be decided, and not at the moment when the provision is actually employed.

The European Constitution: Revision Procedures

Article IV-443: Ordinary Revision Procedure	Article IV-444: Simplified Revision Procedure	Article IV-445: Simplified Revision Procedure Concerning Internal Union Policies and Action
1. The government of any Member State, the European Parliament or the Commission may submit to the Council proposals for the amendment of this Treaty. These proposals shall be submitted to the European Council by the Council and the Parliaments shall be notified.	1. Where Part III provides for the Council to act by unanimity in a given area or case, the European Council may adopt a European decision authorizing the Council to act by a qualified majority in that area or in that case.	1. The Government of any Member State, the European Parliament or the Commission may submit to the European Council proposals for revising all or part of the provisions of Title III of Part III on the internal policies and action of Union.
2. If the European Council, after consulting the European Parliament and the Commission, adopts by a simple majority a decision in favour of examining the proposed amendments, the President of the European Council shall convene a Convention composed of	This paragraph shall not apply to decisions with military implications or those in the area of defence. 2. Where Part III provides for European laws and framework laws to be adopted by the Council in accordance with a special legislative procedure, the European Council may adopt	2. The European Council may adopt a European decision amending all or part of the provisions of Title III of Part III. The European Council shall act by unanimity after consulting the European Parliament and the Commission, and the European Central Bank in

37

The European Constitution: Revision Procedures (Cont'd)

Article IV-443: Ordinary Revision Procedure	Article IV-444: Simplified Revision Procedure	Article IV-445: Simplified Revision Procedure Concerning Internal Union Policies and Action
representatives of the national Parliaments, of the Heads of State or Government of the Member States, of the European Parliament and of the Commission. The European Central Bank shall also be consulted in the case of institutional changes in the monetary area. The Convention shall examine the proposals for amendments and shall adopt by consensus a recommendation to a conference of representatives of the governments of the Member States as provided for in paragraph 3. The European Council may decide by a simple majority, after obtaining the consent of the European Parliament, not to convene a Convention should this not be justified by the extent of the proposed amendments. In the latter case, the European Council shall define the terms of reference for a conference of representatives of govern-ments of the Member States. 3. A conference of representatives of the governments of the Member States shall be convened by the President of the Council for the purpose of determining by common accord the amendments to be made to this Treaty. The amendments shall enter into force after being ratified by all the Member	a European decision allowing for the adoption of such a European laws or frameworks laws in accordance with the ordinary legislative procedure. 3. Any initiative taken by the European Council on the basis of paragraphs 1 or 2 shall be notified to the national Parliaments. If a national Parliament makes known its opposition within six months of the date of such notification, the European decision referred to in paragraphs 1 or 2 shall not be adopted. In the absence of opposition, the European Council may adopt the decision. For the adoption of the European decisions referred to in paragraphs 1 and 2, the European Council shall act by unanimity after obtaining the consent of the European Parliament, which shall be given by a majority of its component members.	case of institutional changes in the monetary area. Such a European decision shall not come into force until it has been approved by the Member States in accordance with their respective constitutional requirements. 3. The European decision referred to in paragraph 2 shall not increase the competences conferred on the Union in this Treaty.

The European Constitution: Revision Procedures (Cont'd)

Article IV-443: Ordinary Revision Procedure	Article IV-444: Simplified Revision Procedure	Article IV-445: Simplified Revision Procedure Concerning Internal Union Policies and Action
States in accordance with their respective constitutional requirements. 4. If, two years after the signature of the treaty amending this Treaty, four fifths of the Member States have ratified it and one or more Member States have encountered difficulties in proceeding with ratification, the matter shall be referred to the European Council.		

Another factor that should be considered is the creation of a President of the European Council (Article I-22 of the Constitution), who will serve a once-renewable term of two and a half years and who will be independent from the Member States in the sense that he or she will not be able to hold a national office, may play a key role in the functioning of the *passerelle* provision and could shape or transform the dynamics of the revision procedures in unpredictable ways.

The procedure set forth in Article IV-445 concerning revisions to Title III of Part III of the Constitution – which is based on a proposal by the Italian Presidency submitted in the Autumn of 2003 – is one of the few appreciable advances made by the IGC in relation to the text it was given by the Convention. As it stands, any changes to the provisions constituting the legal bases of the Union's policies remain subject to a unanimity requirement (despite the urgings of the Commission, for example, which had called for the possibility of revisions based on qualified majority). Nevertheless, the procedure is more streamlined than the ordinary revision procedure foreseen in Article IV-443. Indeed, it is no longer necessary, under the simplified procedure in Article IV-445, to convene an Intergovernmental Conference in order to make revisions. This should facilitate the adoption of selective, limited amendments to the Constitution. By contrast, the convocation of a full-blown IGC has, since the 1980s, often implied a rather wide-ranging agenda leading to extensive negotiations and numerous amendments. Resorting to the IGC not only prolongs the process significantly but above all multiplies the risk that the Member States will start bartering with each other and holding hostage proposals of little concern to them in exchange for support on other proposals affecting their interests. The fact that amendments made to the provisions in Title III of Part III may not increase the Union's competences implies, broadly speaking, that there is no significant risk that national Constitutional Courts will oppose such amendments, or that such amendments might be the subject of national referendums.

All things considered, it does not appear that the Constitution will be so inflexible and impervious to modifications that it will be unable to keep pace with a constantly evolving Europe. At the same time, however, it certainly cannot be said that the various amendment procedures in the Constitution are responsive to the objectives, proclaimed in the Laeken Declaration, of clarification and simplification.

Laeken Declaration of 15 December 2001 (excerpt)

Towards a Constitution for European citizens
The European Union currently has four Treaties. The objectives, powers and policy instruments of the Union are currently spread across those Treaties. If we are to have greater transparency, simplification is essential.

Four sets of questions arise in this connection. The first concerns simplifying the existing Treaties without changing their content. Should the distinction between the Union and the Communities be reviewed? What of the division into three pillars?

Questions then arise as to the possible reorganisation of the Treaties. Should a distinction be made between a basic treaty and the other treaty provisions? Should this distinction involve separating the texts? Could this lead to a distinction between the amendment and ratification procedures for the basic treaty and for the other treaty provisions?

Thought would also have to be given to whether the Charter of Fundamental Rights should be included in the basic treaty and to whether the European Community should accede to the European Convention on Human Rights.

The question ultimately arises as to whether this simplification and reorganisation might not lead in the long run to the adoption of a constitutional text in the Union. What might the basic features of such a constitution be? The values which the Union cherishes, the fundamental rights and obligations of its citizens, the relationship between Member States in the Union?

---

2. ONE TEXT INSTEAD OF TWO

2.1. Replacing the Treaties of Rome and Maastricht

One of the obvious reasons why it is so difficult to understand what the European Union *is* and what it *does* is the coexistence of two Treaties, i.e., the Treaty of Rome of 1957 (establishing the European Community) and the Treaty of Maastricht of 1992 (establishing the European Union), which have different natures and functions. The complexity does not lie in the successive adoption of several different Treaties (including, in addition those just mentioned, the Treaty of Paris of 1951, which expired on 23 July 2002 and thus left coal and steel to be governed by the same internal market and competition rules that apply in other sectors). Indeed, many countries (including certain Member States) with constitutions composed of several different texts have been able to function without serious difficulties. This was the case in France, for example, from 1875 to 1940, and it is still the case in Sweden. Rather, the most salient difficulty in understanding the Union arises from the fact that the Community and the Union, despite sharing the same Member States and Institutions, function according to different principles, rules and procedures. This bifurcation, as it were, is particularly difficult for citizens to grasp, all the more so given that the reasons why the Community is relevant in certain contexts while the Union is relevant in others is far from obvious.

It is little wonder, therefore, that the Laeken Declaration called for a reorganisation and simplification of the Treaties. The questions posed in the Declaration should be kept close when reading the Constitution, in order to evaluate the extent to which those objectives have been achieved.

2.2. The Protocols

The Laeken Declaration made reality seem much more simple than it really is. Even taking account of the fact that the Treaty of Paris expired at the age of 50, the Community and Union frameworks remain highly complex, consisting as they do not only of the Treaties but also of hundreds of international agreements (i.e., protocols) which bind the Member States together and which in fact have the same legal value as the Treaties themselves. To have a complete and detailed picture of the "primary law" of the Community and the Union, i.e., the ultimate source of their powers, it is necessary to take into consideration not only the foundational Treaties, and all of the modifications that have been made to them, but also the Treaties of Accession concluded between the Community/Union and the new Member States with each successive enlargement. To these must be added the voluminous protocols and annexes approved by various Intergovernmental Conferences and ratified together with the Treaties, which confers upon them the same legal value from the standpoint of both Union law and the constitutional laws of the Member States.

Primary law of the European Community and the European Union

Date of signature	Foundational Treaties of the Community and the Union	Entry into force
18 April 1951	Treaty of Paris establishing the European Coal and Steel Community (expired, 23 July 2002) plus 3 annexes and 4 protocols	23 July 1952
25 March 1957	Treaty of Rome establishing the European Economic Community plus 4 annexes, a Convention of execution and 17 protocols	1 January 1958

Primary law of the European Community and the European Union (Cont'd)

Date of signature	Foundational Treaties of the Community and the Union	Entry into force
25 March 1957	Treaty of Rome establishing the European Atomic Community (Euratom) plus 5 annexes and 2 protocols	1 January 1958
7 February 1992	Treaty of Maastricht on European Union plus 17 protocols	1 November 1993
— —	Treaties of Accession	— —
22 January 1972	Denmark, Ireland and the United Kingdom plus an Act relating to the conditions of accession, 11 annexes, 30 protocols and one exchange of letters	1 January 1973
28 May 1979	Greece plus an Act relating to the conditions of accession, 12 annexes and 7 protocols	1 January 1981
12 June 1985	Portugal and Spain plus an Act relating to the conditions of accession, 36 annexes and 25 protocols	1 January 1986
25 June 1994	Austria, Finland and Sweden plus an Act relating to the conditions of accession, 18 annexes and 10 protocols	1 January 1995
10 April 2003	Cyprus, Czech Republic, Estonia, Hungary, Latvia, Lithuania, Malta, Poland Slovakia and Slovenia plus an Act relating to the conditions of accession, 14 annexes and 10 protocols	1 May 2004
— —	Treaties amending the foundational Treaties	— —
8 April 1965	Treaty establishing a single Council and a single Commission of the European Communities ("Merger Treaty") plus 1 protocol	1 July 1967
22 April 1970	Treaty amending certain budgetary provisions of the Treaties	1 January 1971

10 July 1975	Treaty amending the Protocol on the Statute of the European Investment Bank	1 October 1977
22 July 1975	Treaty amending certain financial provisions	1 June 1977
13 March 1984	Treaty amending, with regard to Greenland, the Treaties establishing the European Communities plus 1 protocol	1 February 1985
17-28 February 1986	Single European Act	1 July 1987
7 February 1992	Treaty of Maastricht on European Union plus 17 protocols	1 November 1993
2 October 1997	Treaty of Amsterdam plus 13 protocols	1 May 1999
26 February 1992	Treaty of Nice plus 4 protocols	1 February 2003

The Treaties have also been modified four times by means of "decisions" adopted in accordance with provisions of the Treaties themselves (e.g., the Act concerning the election of representatives of the Assembly [i.e., the European Parliament] by direct universal suffrage, a decision of 20 September 1976).

Many protocols have been of a transitory nature, in particular those annexed to the Treaty of Rome establishing the European Economic Community in 1957 and those annexed to the various Treaties of Accession, for example the protocol concerning tariffs on the importation of bananas of 1957, which expired on 31 December 1992. However, others contain important permanent provisions, such as protocols: establishing the Statute of the Court of Justice (1951, amended in 2001); on the European Central Bank (1992); on special arrangements for Greenland (1985); on the acquisition of property in Denmark (1992); and on the Schengen Agreement (1997). In addition, there are more than 120 declarations adopted by the Intergovernmental Conferences intended to clarify the interpretation to be given to the Treaties and protocols.

Those members of the Convention and its Secretariat who were conscious of the Community/Union's enormous body of primary law understood from the beginning that to revisit and rework these numerous texts would have been like cleaning the stables of King Augeias. However, the scope of such a task was not appreciated by most of the Convention's participants, and the Praesidium opted, in the end, for a solution that merely deferred the problem. Article IV-2 of the Convention's text (*Repeal of earlier Treaties*) provides that:

The Treaty establishing the European Community, the Treaty on European Union *and the acts and treaties which have supplemented or amended them and are listed in the Protocol annexed to the Treaty establishing the Constitution* shall be repealed as from the date of entry into force of the Treaty establishing the Constitution. (emphasis supplied).

Since the Convention did not present any proposed text for the Proposal referred to in Article IV-2, it fell to the legal experts of the Member States during the ICG to identify which texts currently in force will be abrogated. Consequently there were, adjacent to the provisional text of the Constitution of June 2004, two other constituent parts: one of 350 pages containing 36 protocols plus 2 annexes and another of 89 pages containing 39 declarations. Of particular interest among these documents is an explanatory memorandum concerning the Charter of Fundamental Rights, which will undoubtedly be, as many have noted, a "precious instrument of interpretation" for courts. The explanatory memorandum alone occupies 50 pages.

This state of affairs can serve only to accentuate the "masculine" side of the text, that is to say its identity as an international treaty flanked by dozens of other agreements which have exactly the same legal value, even though, symbolically – one might even say morally – these other agreements are of lesser importance than the Constitution.

The problem of the protocols and annexes technically could have been solved if the concept of *organic laws* had been incorporated in the Constitution. An "organic" law is a normative instrument found, for example, in the French Constitution of 1958 or the Spanish Constitution of 1978. It is adopted by means of a more complex procedure than that employed to enact ordinary legislation and accordingly enjoys a superior hierarchical rank. In France, organic laws are also noteworthy in that they are automatically subject to the control of the *Conseil constitutionnel*, which may strike down the measure prior to its entry into force if it contains provisions contrary to the French Constitution.

Two working groups of the Convention, i.e., Working Groups III (*legal personality*) and IX (*simplification*), briefly discussed the possibility of introducing an organic law mechanism into the Constitution. Such a solution was also suggested by certain experts speaking at the Convention, in particular as an alternative device for adopting the quasi-legislative provisions contained in Part III of the text.

Such instruments could have been very useful for adopting the substance of the various protocols and annexes without bestowing upon them the same legal dignity as the Constitution itself. That is, they would have ensured that those acts had the status not of international treaties but rather of legal acts internal to the Union. Organic laws would also have been the most appropriate instrument for the detailed institutional provisions found in Chapter I, Title VI of Part III of the Constitution.

Nevertheless, the concept of organic laws was discarded, partly on the ground that it was too complicated. A golden opportunity was thus unfortunately missed, and it is disappointing that the Member States did not make a more earnest effort in this regard. If they were concerned about being able to veto any amendments to such internal legal acts, they could have accomplished this merely by establishing a unanimity requirement for the European Council.

2.3. Tabula Rasa not an Option

The substitution of one Constitution by another superseding the last is a rather common phenomenon. Often such reforms are simply a matter of redrafting an aging text in more contemporary language, as was done in Finland and Switzerland in 2000 and in The Netherlands in 1983. In other cases, the process is more complex because it corresponds to a change of the political regime. Italy found itself in this situation in 1947. In Germany, such reforms occurred in 1919 and in 1949. Portugal also went through at least two regime changes, in 1910 and especially in 1976. Spain went through more than six, the last of which was in 1978. And in France, regimes came and went no less than 16 times between 1791 and 1958! Moreover, since the fall of the Berlin wall in November of 1989, nearly all of the countries in Central and Eastern Europe have completely overhauled their respective constitutions.

Where constitutional reform has coincided with regime change, certain countries have also seized the opportunity to repeal some of the ousted regime's legislation. However, in most cases, pre-existing legislation has in fact remained in force and the newly prevailing Constitutions have simply provided for the possibility of challenging its constitutionality before the national Constitutional Courts. The clearest example of this is the Italian Constitution of 1947, which established a procedure for *preliminary references* that subsequently served as a model for the European Community's own well-known preliminary reference procedure (Article 234, ex-177 of the Treaty of Rome) whereby national courts may (and sometimes must) refer to the Court of Justice questions concerning the interpretation of Community law.

However, in the case of the European Constitution, it was not possible to merely leave the extant protocols and annexes in place with the possibility of challenging them before the European Courts. The reason why such a solution could not be adopted may be explained by reference to the particularities of the *legal bases* that are available to the Institutions of the Union.

A sovereign State by definition is competent to legislate in any field it chooses. The only question to be settled by the constitution of a State with a unitary structure is whether the parliament is to have the exclusive right to enact legally binding rules or whether, in certain defined cases, the government will also be entrusted with legislative functions. If a unitary State is transformed into a federal State, as in the case of Austria in 1920, one need only consult the new constitution to determine whether amendments to pre-existing legislation are to be adopted by that national parliament or the sub-national legislator. In either case, the legislation can continue to subsist without any particular difficulty.

By contrast, the Community and the Union can only legislate when the Treaties recognise a legal basis attributing legislative powers to them in relation to specified fields. This notion of limited powers is known as the *principle of conferral*, and it is clearly expressed in Articles I-1(1) and especially I-11(2) of the Constitution. The latter provision states that:

> Under the principle of conferral, the Union shall act within the limits of the competences conferred upon it by the Member States in the Constitution to attain the objectives set out in the Constitution. Competences not conferred upon the Union in the Constitution remain with the Member States.

The principle of conferral implies that, once the Treaties are repealed, the legal bases contained in them must be maintained to avoid the "re-nationalisation" of a whole series of competences with which the Community and the Union have already been entrusted. Indeed, if these legal bases were not preserved, then the Union's Institutions would lose not only their power to legislate but also their ability to apply the legislation and regulatory rules of the Community and the Union that are already in place. Moreover, the legal bases prescribed in the Treaties constitute a significant part of Union law because the Court of Justice considers them, under certain conditions, to be *directly applicable*, i.e., that they are binding and may be directly relied on in court proceedings. Such legal bases may thus be relied on, in particular, in legal actions challenging national legislation on the ground that it fails to respect such provisions.

The Convention therefore faced a dilemma that has been the subject of much reflection on the part of commentators. The goals of simplification and reorganisation of the Treaties, as set forth in the Laeken Declaration, seemed to call for the adoption of a text as short and simple as possible, i.e., it seemed to call for a text unburdened by the more complicated provisions contained in the existing Treaties setting down legal bases. On the other hand, a text limited to short, simple statements risked being little more than a declaratory document without any real "teeth". Furthermore, if the Constitution had failed to carry over those legal bases from the Treaties, this would have been truly revolutionary because it would have reallocated to the Member States a host of competences that they had already conferred, in some cases as far back as 1958, upon the Community and the Union.

In any event, the Convention was given neither the mandate nor the political authority necessary to conduct a complete re-examination of the division of the various fields of action between the European and the national levels. The most it could do was to propose marginal adjustments, in particular by inserting certain new legal bases in Part III, for example in matters of civil protection. The fires that devastated Europe during the summer of 2003, shortly after the definitive adoption of the Convention's draft, amply demonstrated the utility of a device allowing for reinforced and simplified cooperation between Member States in that field.

3. Four Parts Distinguished According to Their Content, Origins and Elaboration

3.1. The Price of Clarification: 448 Articles instead of 434

The text consigned to the European Council at the summit in Thessaloniki on 20 June 2003 was in fact short, handy and easy to read. It consisted of a Preamble and 59 Articles plus the Charter of Fundamental Rights, which in turn contained a Preamble and 54 Articles, and two protocols.

From a quantitative point of view, therefore, the text presented at Thessaloniki could easily be compared, say, to the Italian Constitution of 1947 (139 Articles, of which 54 are devoted to fundamental principles and to the rights and duties of citizens, plus 28 transitory and final provisions), or to the French Constitution of 1958 (89 Articles, which must be read together with the 17 Articles of the Declaration of the Rights of Man and of the Citizen of 1789 and the 16 paragraphs of the Preamble to the Constitution of 1946). For its part, the German Fundamental Law is composed of 179 Articles, including 19 provisions on fundamental rights which are supplemented by 5 Articles of the Weimar Constitution that remain in force. Indeed, the text presented to the Council is a model of concision compared to the Austrian Constitution. The latter text consists of six constitutional laws – not counting the law concerning Austria's accession to the Union – the first of which alone contains more than 200 Articles. Many of these provisions take up the space of an entire chapter of the Thessaloniki text!

The Convention had made a deliberate effort, in Parts I and II, to forge a text at once readable and precise. However, these two virtues are not always mutually compatible. Although these first two Parts convey a good idea about what the Union is and what it does, they are not sufficient to specify clearly the powers of the Union's Institutions, particularly in relation to the dividing line between the Union's competences and the competences reserved exclusively to the Member States. Nor do they precisely indicate the rights recognised by the Constitution in favour of the Union's citizens, citizens of third countries residing in a Member State, enterprises and associations.

Considering the constraints under which the Convention carried out its work, the expanded text of 18 July 2003, which included Parts III and IV and amounted to 465 Articles plus five protocols, can be said to have remained within reasonable limits. Indeed, it should not be forgotten that the Constitution had to replace, without distorting the contents of, not only the 317 Articles of the Treaty of Rome (i.e., the EC Treaty) and the 63 Articles of the Treaty of Maastricht (Treaty on European Union) but also the 54 Articles of the Charter of Fundamental Rights (i.e., a total of 434 Articles). In the end, the text adopted by the IGC in Brussels on 18 June 2004 and signed in Rome on 29 October of the same year contained 448 Articles, as the legal experts preparing the IGC managed to fold a certain number of provisions into others with which they were logically linked. Accompanying the text are 36 protocols and 42 annexes, as opposed to the hundreds currently attached to the Treaties. The final result is still too much for a Constitution; nevertheless, a great deal has been achieved in terms of clarification.

An increase of only 14 Articles in fact represents a significant success, particularly since the Convention did not resort to the chicanery often used by constituent assemblies, such as packing multiple provisions into one composite provision subdivided into numerous sections. In this case, the additions that were made corresponded to new provisions, serving in nearly each instance to clarify complex Articles, to establish new legal bases or to introduce other innovations.

Furthermore, the Constitution is pieced together much more logically than the Treaties. This can be seen clearly from the fact that if one wished to find all of the provisions governing the Union's Institutions today, it would be necessary to consult both the Treaty of Rome and the Treaty of Maastricht. Even more tellingly, one would have to read the Treaty of Maastricht to determine how to amend the Treaty of Rome! This situation was not only inconvenient and intransparent, it also created the potential for incoherence or even contradictions between the corresponding provisions of the two Treaties.

3.2. Part I: The Constitutional Provisions

Part I of the Convention's text contained a number of signs intended to alert the reader that the document was a Constitution for Europe with a capital *C*:
- in contrast to the other three Parts, Part I did not have a title, as indeed, any title other than "Constitution" would have been inappropriate;
- unlike the other Parts, the Articles contained in Part I were numbered from 1 to 59 without being preceded by a Roman numeral – although the IGC decided instead to number the text continuously from Article 1 to Article 448, using Roman numerals to indicate the corresponding Part of the text, including Part I (e.g., Article I-29);

- most of the wording used in the provisions of Part I is new (as is equally the case in the final text) and was formulated following debate in the Convention's working groups and in its plenary sessions; this applied both in the case of novel legal questions and where the Convention was enshrining principles culled from the jurisprudence of the Court of Justice;
- the order of the new Titles contained in Part I was dictated by two primary concerns, didactic and juridical in nature: on the one hand it had to be made clear what the Union does (and what it can do) before the Institutions, and the procedures enabling them to act, could be presented; on the other hand, it was necessary to set forth the principles that will guide the Institutions in the interpretation and execution of the Constitution's provisions, making European citizenship as meaningful as possible and elevating it above the economically-oriented freedoms that have dominated European integration for the past 50 years.

European Constitution

Part I

TITLE I: DEFINITION AND OBJECTIVES OF THE UNION

Article I-1: Establishment of the Union

Article I-2: The Union's values

Article I-3: The Union's objectives

Article I-4: Fundamental freedoms and non-discrimination

Article I-5: Relations between the Union and the Member States

Article I-6: Union law

Article I-7: Legal personality

Article I-8: The symbols of the Union

TITLE II: FUNDAMENTAL RIGHTS AND CITIZENSHIP OF THE UNION

Article I-9: Fundamental rights

Article I-10: Citizenship of the Union

TITLE III: UNION COMPETENCES

Article I-11: Fundamental principles

Article I-12: Categories of competence

Article I-13: Areas of exclusive competence

Article I-14: Areas of shared competence

Article I-15: The coordination of economic and employment policies

Article I-16: The common foreign and security policy

Article I-17: Areas of supporting, coordinating or complementary action

Article I-18: Flexibility clause

TITLE IV: THE UNION'S INSITUTIONS AND BODIES

CHAPTER I – THE INSTITUTIONAL FRAMEWORK

Article I-19: The Union's institutions

European Constitution (Cont'd)

European Constitution (Cont'd)

Article I-52: Status of churches and non-confessional organisations

TITLE VII: THE UNION'S FINANCES
Article I-53: Budgetary and financial principles
Article I-54: The Union's own resources
Article I-55: The multiannual financial framework
Article I-56: The Union's budget

TITLE VIII: THE UNION AND ITS NEIGHBOURS
Article I-57: The Union and its neighbours

TITLE IX: UNION MEMBERSHIP
Article I-58: Conditions of eligibility and procedure for accession to the Union
Article I-59: Suspension of certain rights resulting from Union membership
Article I-60: Voluntary withdrawal from the Union

All of the Treaties, from the Treaty of Paris onward, were founded on the establishment of certain *objectives*, as is demonstrated in particular by Article 3 of the Treaty of Rome. However, the common *values* of the Union were never defined, despite the fact that the expression was introduced in Article 11 (ex-Article J-1) of the Treaty of Maastricht and since 1997 has appeared in the Treaty of Rome as well. In the Constitution, the Union's values are set forth in Article I-2. (see page 5).

Part I of the Constitution carries over the objectives from the Treaties, condensing them and developing them to promote principles that could not be inserted in Article I-2, either for reasons of style or due to the fact that Article I-2 is intended to specify only those values for which a "clear risk of a serious breach" may lead to the suspension of a Member State's rights under Article I-59.

The values, principles and objectives contained in the Constitution are of diverse origin. First, some of them had already appeared explicitly in the Treaty of Maastricht. A second source was the case law of the Court of Justice. Others derived from legal instruments that have been adopted on the basis of the Treaties. Finally, some were expressed for the first time during the proceedings of the Convention.

Debates within the Convention sometimes reached fever pitch. The question of what should and should not be regarded as a *value* is highly subjective and is conditioned by cultural factors such as national heritage, professional background, diplomatic experience, etc. To respond to the strong claims that continued to be made following the conclusion of the Convention, the IGC in the end decided to incorporate, in Article I-2, references to equality between women and men and to the respect for the rights of persons belonging to minorities. The impact of the precise wording that appears in Article I-2 will depend in large part on how the formulations are used in practice by the Institutions and, above all, on how they are interpreted by the Court of Justice.

The text of the Constitution, and particularly Part I, must be read in light of the Constitution's dual character: that of a Constitution, written for the citizen; and that of a treaty whose aim is to consolidate the values and principles already accumulated in the Treaties which it is destined to replace.

3.3. Part II: The Charter of Fundamental Rights of the Union

The origins of Part II of the Constitution, which consists of the Charter of Fundamental Rights, are very different from those of Part I. Practically the entire text of Part II was in fact drafted by an earlier Convention that carried out its work in 1999-2000, following which the Charter was "solemnly proclaimed" at the Nice summit on 7 December 2000 (see the table at page 7).

With respect to the Charter, the Laeken Declaration was clear: "Thought would also have to be given to whether the Charter of Fundamental Rights should be included in the basic treaty and to whether the European Community should accede to the European Convention on Human Rights". From this it can be seen that the European Convention was not called on to tinker with the Charter, which was not only the result of careful and thorough elaboration but also the product of delicate compromises. Moreover, work on the Charter by the Convention of 1999-2000 had only been accepted by detractors and allowed to proceed after assurances were made that the Charter would have no binding legal force for quite some time. Thus, whatever opinion one may have about this or that provision of the Charter, it must be understood that for the European Convention of 2002-2003, the only options with regard to the existing text was to take it or leave it.

From the quotation above it can be seen that the Laeken Declaration raised three essential issues in relation to human rights protection. The first and easiest matter to resolve was whether the Union should accede to the European Convention on Human Rights (to which all of the countries represented at the Convention had already subscribed). In an Opinion delivered in 1996, the Court of Justice had concluded that the Treaty of Rome in fact did not permit accession and that the Union therefore could not accede unless the Treaty were amended to provide an explicit basis for such a move.

The question of accession to the ECHR has now been settled by Article I-9(2) of the Constitution, which provides that "[t]he Union shall accede to the European Convention for the Protection of Human Rights and Fundamental Freedoms". As a technical matter, since the Union is not a State, the 46 States that belong to the Council of Europe (i.e., the regional institution responsible for the promulgation of and respect for the ECHR) must agree to make the necessary adjustments to the ECHR before the accession of the Union can become a reality. In the meantime, lawyers will be able to reflect on how to fashion mechanisms and rules that will foster a harmonious interrelationship between the legal systems and institutions of the ECHR and those of the Union.

A second issue raised by the Laeken Declaration in the human rights context concerned the possibility of making the Charter of Fundamental Rights legally binding. The governments that had originally opposed this idea at the Nice summit in 2000 did not really have a change of heart during the Convention of 2002-2003. However, the Convention's dynamics were such that it became politically impossible for those governments to maintain their position, which indeed clashed with that of the vast majority of the members of the Convention. If those governments had remained obstinate, those in the majority certainly would not have hesitated to get the international press harping on the theme of their lack of democratic spirit.

But the game was not to be so easily won. The Charter faced criticism from all sides, including notably from university professors, who disagreed with the Charter's formulation, or who feared that its adoption could impede subsequent developments in the jurisprudence of the Court of Justice in the field of fundamental rights. Despite these challenges, however, the working group charged with examining the possibility of transforming the Charter into a binding set of principles did not have difficulty finding the consensus necessary to reach the most transparent solution, i.e., the actual incorporation of the Charter in the text of the Constitution. Forming part of the text itself, the Charter was thus elevated to the rank of binding legal norms that will be "justiciable" before courts and hence enforceable. The so-called "horizontal clauses" contained in Articles II-111 (*Field of application*) and II-112 (*Scope and interpretation of rights and principles*), to which the United Kingdom clung tightly and which could only arouse passion in the hearts of lawyers, do not change the fact that the Charter will have binding force, as the horizontal clauses merely spell out the consequences of Charter's underlying legal logic. As for the bizarre references (in the fifth paragraph of the Charter's Preamble and in Article II-112(7)) to the explanatory memorandum prepared for the Praesidium of the Convention of 1999-2000 (and further refined by the Convention of 2002-2003) – which were the result of a rear guard action by the British government – their main effect is to weigh down the style of the Preamble that that first Convention had so carefully crafted. Furthermore, the explanatory memorandum itself adds considerably to the bulk of the declarations annexed to the Constitution. There is no doubt that Courts will be obliged to give "due regard" to the explanations when interpreting the Charter. However, in most cases these explanations simply recall the origin of the rights embraced therein, whether it be Treaty provisions, secondary law, the ECHR, the European Social Charter, or the case law of the Court of Justice.

The third human rights-related issue was whether the Charter should be inserted in the actual text of the Constitution (and if so, where) or whether it should instead be attached to the text as a protocol. Here again there was a kind of coalition between the Charter's detractors and certain legal experts, who emphasised the difficulties that would arise from the articulation of certain rights twice in the same constitutional text. However, the wisdom of incorporating the Charter in the Constitution itself can be seen from the French experience. In France, the legally binding catalogue of fundamental rights is comprised of both the Declaration of the Rights of Man and of the Citizen of 1789 and the Preamble to the Constitution of 1946. However, while both texts are considered to be integral parts of the Constitution of 1958, they are not always published together with that text, which leads to significant confusion on the part of common citizens.

The official decision of whether to incorporate the Charter in the Constitution was postponed to the last minute, undoubtedly to avoid creating any pretext for a fresh debate on its legally binding nature. But when the Praesidium made its choice in the spring of 2003, it was by that time obvious that the text would be incomplete without the Charter. The text delivered to the Council in Thessaloniki thus, in the end, contained highly visible guarantees of the broad range of fundamental rights protecting the people.

3.4. Part III: Consolidation of the Legal Bases and the Detailed Institutional Provisions Concerning the Policies and Functioning of the Union

At the time of the Thessaloniki Summit of 20 June 2003, Part III of the Convention's text, *The Policies and Functioning of the Union*, had not yet been finalised. On the other hand, even if the text had been ready, it may just as well have been wise for the President of the Convention to delay the presentation of it anyway: critics would have wasted no time attacking the 342 Articles contained in Part III as being bloated, sometimes inelegant, and gratuitously complex.

The Laeken Council had asked the Convention to reflect on a "possible reorganisation of the Treaties". Such an undertaking was then carefully considered by Working Group III ("Legal personality") and by the Praesidium. In particular, they aimed their efforts at answering three questions raised by the Laeken Declaration.

First, the Declaration asked: "Should a distinction be made between a basic treaty and the other treaty provisions?" In essence, the Convention responded affirmatively: the basic provisions are included in Part I, while the other more supplementary and technical provisions appear in Parts III and IV. This distinction is not merely of didactic interest, but has real legal consequences. Indeed, the provisions contained in Part III will have to be applied in the light of Part I, and in the light of the Charter. Given the truly constitutional nature of these basic provisions, it can be expected that in the future this will lead to an interpretation of Part III that is based on more than strictly economic criteria.

The second question posed by the Declaration was: "Should this distinction involve separating the texts?" At the request of the Commission, in 2000 a group of experts from the European University Institute (EUI) in Florence, Italy, had already worked on a proposed text that was divided into two parts, a "basic treaty" (an allusion to Germany's Basic Law) and a second, supplementary treaty. Many among the EUI experts, including the author of this book, considered that the proposal presented to the Commission had the advantage of demonstrating the feasibility of a reorganisation of the Treaties, yet were unconvinced that the division of the texts into two distinct Treaties would respond to the need for simplification. The Convention's reasoning seems to have been similar, given that it separated the fundamental provisions from the technical ones without creating two separate texts.

Third: could such a separation of the texts "lead to a distinction between the amendment and ratification procedures for the basic treaty and for the other treaty provisions?" Although the experts from the EUI had already been asked to address this issue, they managed to sidestep the question in their report. The question of amendments and ratification makes it necessary to consider the relative importance of the provisions of the Treaties.

Two kinds of criteria (which do not usually overlap) may be employed to measure the importance of those provisions. The criteria that refer to EU citizenship and to the symbols of the Union make it possible to separate the principles from the corresponding provisions of application without great effort. However, there are other criteria, linked to the delimitation of powers between the Union and the Member States, which present more serious difficulties. For example, the matter of whether a vote by the Council is to be subject to qualified majority voting or to unanimity is obviously a technical question; yet it is also essential for defining the powers of the Member States. Such criteria thus would have led to a number of complex incisions in most of the provisions of the Treaties of Rome and of Maastricht. The task would also have been exhausting, and very political given that some legal bases are considered to be fundamental by certain Member States but not by others. This implies that an undertaking of that kind could not have been delegated to legal experts, and likely would have monopolised the Convention's time without any guarantee of coherent and legible results. The Italian proposal adopted by the IGC (Article IV-445), which envisages a simplified procedure for making certain amendments to the Constitution provided they do not result in an expansion of the competences of the Union, has the virtue of simplicity. It does not solve all the problems related to constitutional amendments; however, it avoids sterile political debates positing hypothetical scenarios.

The primary characteristic of Part III is that it reproduces the content of many of the technical provisions of the Treaties of Rome and of Maastricht. However, Part III also rearranges the order of those provisions to give a clearer picture of what the Union can do.

Subsection 7: The Court of Auditors
Section 2: The Union's advisory bodies
    Subsection 1: The Committee of the Regions
    Subsection 2: The Economic and Social Committee
Section 3: The European Investment Bank
Section IV: Provisions common to Union Institutions, bodies, offices and agencies
CHAPTER II – FINANCIAL PROVISIONS
Section 1: The mutiannual financial framework
Section 2: The Union's annual budget
Section 3: Implementation of the budget and discharge
Section 4: Common provisions
Section 5: Combating fraud
CHAPTER III – ENHANCED COOPERATION
TITLE IV: COMMON PROVISIONS

With respect to the Union's policies, the reorganisation of the relevant provisions follows two complementary lines of logic. Firstly, an attempt was made to arrange the provisions from the most important to the least important in terms of the intensity of the Union's actions. Secondly, the provisions in Part III concerning individuals are placed ahead of the more economically-oriented provisions (most notably those pertaining to the internal market), whereas in the Treaty of Rome it is the other way around.

Provisions Relating to the Internal Market
in the Treaty of Rome and in the Convention's Text

Treaty of Rome	Convention text
PART III: COMMUNITY POLICIES TITLE I: FREE MOVEMENT OF GOODS	TITLE III: INTERNAL POLICIES AND ACTION
CHAPTER I – CUSTOMS UNION CHAPTER II – PROHIBITION OF QUANTITATIVE RESTRICTIONS BETWEEN MEMBER STATES	CHAPTER 1 – INTERNAL MARKET Section 1 – Establishment of the Internal Market
TITLE II: AGRICULTURE	Section 2 – Free Movement of Persons and Services

TITLE III: FREE MOVEMENT OF PERSONS, SERVICES AND CAPITAL
CHAPTER I – WORKERS
CHAPTER II – RIGHT OF ESTABLISHMENT
CHAPTER III – SERVICES
CHAPTER IV – CAPITAL AND PAYMENTS
	Subsection 1 – Workers
	  Subsection 2 – Freedom of establishment
	  Subsection 3 – Freedom to provide services
	Section 3 – Free Movement of Goods
	  Subsection 1 – Customs union

*Provisions Relating to the Internal Market in the
Treaty of Rome and in the Convention's Text* (Cont'd)

Treaty of Rome	Convention text
TITLE IV: VISAS, ASYLUM, IMMIGRATION AND OTHER POLICIES RELATED TO FREE MOVEMENT OF PERSONS	Subsection 2 – Customs cooperation Subsection 3 – Prohibition of quantitative restrictions
TITLE V: TRANSPORT	Section 4 – Capital and Payments
TITLE VI: COMMON RULES ON COMPETITION, TAXATION AND APPROXIMATION OF LAWS CHAPTER I – RULES ON COMPETITION CHAPTER II – TAX PROVISIONS CHAPTER III – APPROXIMATION OF LAWS	Section 5 – Rules on Competition Subsection 1 – Rules applying to undertakings Subsection 2 – Aids granted by Member Section 6 – Fiscal Provisions Section 7 – Approximation of Legislation

As can be seen from the table above, the Convention placed the principle of free movement of persons and services ahead of the principle of free movement of goods, whereas in the Treaty of Rome these principles were laid down in the opposite order. The Constitution retained this significant change of emphasis.

It is also noteworthy that the reorganised texts contained in Part III are not mere replicas of their original counterparts, but rather include a number of significant changes:
- Nearly all of the Articles have been partially rewritten to adapt them to the newly classified legal instruments and procedures, as set forth in Part I;
- Many Articles have been entirely rewritten, replaced, or supplemented by new provisions so as to integrate proposals made by the working groups and "discussion circles" of the Convention with a view toward improving the functioning of the Union and its Institutions. The ICG also introduced a certain number of new provisions, in particular general provisions that reinforce those concerning citizenship and the Union's social dimension. In addition, a new Article III-115 has been incorporated, which states that "[t]he Union shall ensure consistency between the policies and activities referred to in [Part III], taking all of its objectives into account and in accordance with the principle of conferral of powers."
- To ensure a solid foundation for policies that the Member States and the Commission had already begun to develop, a number of new legal bases have been inserted. In this respect, the Constitution follows in the tradition of the Single European Act and the Treaties of Maastricht, Amsterdam and Nice.

3.5. Part IV: General and Final Provisions

Constitutions and international treaties routinely contain a certain number of general and final provisions. Some provisions included in the European Constitution are typical of international treaties, such as the definition of the scope of application of the Constitution in space (Article IV-440, which covers territorial scope) and in time (Article IV-446, providing for an unlimited duration). Such provisions are not normally included in constitutions. Other provisions appear which are common to constitutions and treaties alike, for example those concerning the Constitution's entry into force (Article IV-447), the conditions for amendment (Articles IV-443 to IV-445), transitional arrangements (Articles IV-438 and IV-439), the legal value of the protocols and annexes (Article IV-442) and the authentic languages in which the text is written (Article IV-448).

European Constitution

Part IV: General and Final Provisions

Article IV-437: Repeal of earlier Treaties

Article IV-438: Succession and legal continuity

Article IV-439: Transitional provisions relating to certain institutions

Article IV-440: Scope

Article IV-441: Regional unions

Article IV-442: Protocols and Annexes

Article IV-443: Ordinary revision procedure

Article IV-444: Simplified revision procedure

Article IV-445: Simplified revision procedure concerning internal Union policies and action

Article IV-446: Duration

Article IV-447: Ratification and entry into force

Article IV-448: Authentic texts and translations

The differences between the general and final provisions of the Constitution and those of the Treaties of Rome and of Maastricht are of little significance. In general, the provisions of the Constitution are comparatively brief, but that is due to the fact that the reorganisation of the original provisions led to the relocation of certain parts of those provisions to other, more logical places in the text. Rather than applying the "kitchen sink" approach and haphazardly including miscellaneous provisions (such as those, for example, in Articles 281-314 of the Treaty of Rome), Part IV of the Constitution is limited to genuinely "general and final" provisions.

Certain provisions of particular importance were the focus of intense discussions during the proceedings of the Convention and the ICG. On the one hand, there were the provisions that ultimately became Articles IV-443, IV-444 and IV-445, which relate to procedures for amending the Constitution, and on the other hand there was the provision concerning ratification and entry into force, which is contained in Article IV-447. In the end, the Convention and the IGC decided that discretion was the better part of valour, and the final versions of those provisions, while featuring some interesting innovations, do not represent a break with the past.

The final note regarding Part IV is the icing on the cake. The provisions relating to the symbols of the Union (i.e., the flag, the anthem, the currency, etc.) had been suggested by certain members of the Convention only after the Thessaloniki summit, and, as it was therefore too late to insert them in Part I, they were relegated to the obscure backwaters of Article IV-1 of the Convention's text. However, the IGC rectified this incongruity and the symbols found their rightful home in Article I-8, at the end of the first Title of Part I.

3.6. The Protocols and Declarations Annexed to the Constitution

It often happens that constitutions and treaties are accompanied by other, more detailed annexes whose tone and length would be inappropriate if they were incorporated as part of the principal text. However, as these annexes are approved together with the text in question, in accordance with the same national procedures, they attain the same legal value as the text itself.

Annexes of this kind, particularly in the context of European integration, are generally called "protocols". To ensure a sufficiently smooth and coherent text, it was inevitable that a number of such annexes would flank the Constitution rather than being integrated in the text itself. However, the term "protocol" has the disadvantage of making clear to the reader that the text is yet another international treaty. It was no accident that, in the so-called "Penelope" working document, which was presented to the Convention in January of 2003 in the name of Commission President Romano Prodi (although not the Commission itself) and which amounted to a proposed draft Constitution, the annexes were named "Additional Acts".

In any case, since the idea of incorporating organic laws was discarded (see pages 44–45), and since the provisions concerning amendments to the text are more typical of a treaty than a Constitution, the term "protocol" will have to suffice. At least it can be said that, in contrast to the Treaties of Maastricht and of Amsterdam, the number of protocols annexed to the Constitution cannot be regarded as an abuse.

Protocols and declarations annexed to the Convention's text

---

1. Protocol on the role of national Parliaments in the European Union
2. Protocol on the application of the principles of subsidiarity and proportionality
3. Protocol on the representation of citizens in the European Parliament and the weighting of votes in the European Council and the Council of Ministers
4. Protocol on the Euro Group
5. Protocol amending the Euratom Treaty

1. Declaration attached to the Protocol on the representation of citizens in the European Parliament and the weighting of votes in the European Council and the Council of Ministers
2. Declaration on the creation of a European External Action Service
3. Declaration in the final act of signature of the Treaty establishing the Constitution

---

The first two protocols attached to the Convention's text were the Protocol on the role of national Parliaments in the European Union and the Protocol on the application of the principles of subsidiarity and proportionality. These protocols, which closely resemble organic laws, introduce some important innovations *vis-à-vis* their predecessors, originally adopted as part of the Treaty of Amsterdam.

The third protocol was the Protocol on the representation of citizens in the European Parliament and the weighting of votes in the European Council and the Council of Ministers. A typical product of agreements reached hastily in the waning hours of the EU's Intergovernmental Conferences, this protocol contains provisions considered necessary in June of 2003 to make certain institutional innovations easier to swallow, particularly for Spain and Poland. These provisions are of a transitory character and the protocol is set to expire on 1 November 2009.

The fourth protocol, also of a transitory nature but without a fixed duration, was the Protocol on the Euro Group, i.e., the group of Member States whose currency is the Euro. This protocol provides for an embryonic economic governance (i.e., an "ever-closer coordination of economic policies") of the Union, without bestowing any specific powers, in the anticipation that all the Member States will ultimately adopt the Euro. The protocol further anticipates that all the Member States will accept the idea of an economic governance body at the supranational level, which many consider to be an important institutional "partner" of the European Central Bank in the management of economic policy. The latter view is, however, far from unanimous among the Member State governments.

The fifth protocol was the Protocol amending the Euratom Treaty, which does not pertain directly to the Constitution as such. In the beginning the idea had been to integrate the terms of the Euratom Treaty into the new Constitution, but this proposal was opposed by the Greens, who regard Euratom as incompatible with an acceptable environmental policy. According to the compromise that emerged, Euratom will continue to subsist as an independent organisation with particular links to the Union and to the Member States. Considering the limited political and economic impact of Euratom for the Member States in the 21st Century, such a solution can scarcely be viewed as controversial.

The three declarations proposed by the Convention, far fewer in number than those generally agreed by the Intergovernmental Conferences, are not intended to produce actual legal effects. Nevertheless, they are significant insofar as they reflect delicate compromises and they should be studied in parallel with the provisions of the Constitution to which they correspond. Of particular importance is the Declaration in the final act of signature of the Treaty establishing the Constitution, which provides for the possibility of intervention by the European Council in case of non-ratification and which could conceivably lead to significant changes to the Constitution.

The Convention did not venture to modify the protocols and declarations annexed to the existing Treaties. It took more than six months for the legal experts of the

Council and the Commission, in collaboration with other lawyers representing the Member States, to take inventory of these texts and to decide which ones had become obsolete and which ones remained necessary for the functioning of the Union and for the maintenance of certain specific provisions. In the end, these experts drew up one list of 36 protocols and two annexes, plus another list of 39 declarations, all to be annexed to the final text. By the time the Constitution was signed in Rome on 29 October 2004, the number of declarations had grown to 50. All of the other texts not carried over from the Treaties will expire when the Constitution enters into force. This will contribute enormously to legal certainty and will simplify the work of practitioners. The work of the experts demonstrates once again that it would have been better to introduce the possibility of using organic laws to induct the necessary protocols and declarations into the new regime. Instead, unless otherwise indicated in the Constitution, the modification of these texts will be subject to the ordinary and relatively cumbersome revision procedures.

4. One Text; at Least 21 Languages

The very last provision of the Constitution, Article IV-448 (*Authentic texts and translations*), rightly recalls Europe's multicultural nature and names the twenty-one languages, from Czech to Swedish, in which authentic texts of the Constitution appear. In maintaining authentic texts covering the official languages of all the Member States, the Constitution carries on in the tradition of the existing Treaties. Despite criticisms from the populist press concerning the costs of a system requiring that all generally applicable legislation and regulations be translated into twenty languages (Gaelic is not used for instruments of "secondary" law), it is quite absurd to portray the Union's multilingual regime as a heavy financial burden, given that translation costs represent only a small part of a budget that is dwarfed by those of the Member States.

Article IV-448

Authentic Texts and Translations

1. This Treaty, drawn up in a single original in the Czech, Danish, Dutch, English, Estonian, Finnish, French, German, Greek, Hungarian, Irish, Italian, Latvian, Lithuanian, Maltese, Polish, Portuguese, Slovak, Slovenian, Spanish and Swedish languages, the texts in each of these languages being equally authentic, shall be deposited in the archives of the Government of the Italian Republic, which will transmit a certified copy to each of the governments of the other signatory States.
2. This Treaty may also be translated into any other languages as determined by Member States among those which, in accordance with their constitutional order, enjoy official status in all or part of their territory. A certified copy of such translations shall be provided by the Member States concerned to be deposited in the archives of the Council.

Furthermore, from the point of view of citizenship and the rule of law, it is indispensable in a complex, multicultural system such as the Union to have authentic, official versions of legislation and of the jurisprudence of the European Courts in multiple languages. First of all, such a multilingual approach is necessary to ensure a uniform application of Union law – a principle not specifically mentioned in the Constitution but an inherent part of the principle of primacy of Union law over the law of the Member States, which is articulated in Article I-6 (*Union law*). An approach favouring the most widespread languages would also be inconsistent with the rule against discrimination on the basis of nationality, contained in Article I-4(2), not to mention an explicit guarantee of respect for the Union's cultural and linguistic diversity, which appears in Article I-3(3), fourth paragraph. Moreover, if official translations were not generated by the services of the Union, and at the expense of its budget, the financial burden of producing translations would fall to small Member States whose languages are relatively rare – without any guarantees as to the quality and precision of such translations, nor as to their consistency with translations of corresponding texts generated elsewhere. For these reasons, the Treaties, the jurisprudence of the European Courts and the Constitution are all subject to the principle of absolute equality in respect of the relevant languages and it would be contrary to Union law to privilege any version of a text over the others.

Article IV-448(2) of the Constitution, which was adopted by the IGC on the basis of a proposal of the new Spanish government following the elections of March 2004, allows for the possibility of a Member State to translate the Constitution into any additional language that enjoys official status in all or part of its territory. This provision represents a compromise between, on the one hand, the demands of certain autonomous communities, in particular Catalonia and the Basque Country, and on the other hand the concerns of Member State governments with little enthusiasm for stretching the list of official languages of the Union any further. Although Article IV-448(2) was devised primarily with the Basque, Catalan and Galician languages in mind, it cannot be excluded that, in the future, depending on how the situation evolves in certain Baltic states, other translations will appear, including perhaps even Russian. However, in contrast to the list of twenty-one languages in Article IV-448(1) (which undoubtedly will inherit other languages as the Union continues to expand), translations in other languages falling under Article IV-448(2) will not be formally recognised by the Court of Justice and hence will play no role in the resolution of problems of interpretation of the law of the Union.

That said, the principal critique that may be made with regard to the Convention's final text of 18 July 2003 concerns the uneven quality of the various translations. The plenary sessions of the Convention were always conducted in all eleven official languages of the Union, thanks to the simultaneous interpretation services of the Institutions. Simultaneous interpretation was also provided for some of the languages spoken in the candidate countries participating in the proceedings. However, for obvious reasons of convenience, the languages used for the written work of the Convention were limited to English and French. Although all the contributions presented were translated into at least English and French, this was not always the case for other languages. Nevertheless, whenever it was necessary to formulate the actual drafts of the Constitution, the plenary sessions always had versions available in the eleven official languages.

It is not always possible to know the languages in which the first drafts of the Convention's text were written, but it is clear that, in general, French was the dominant language used. This can be seen from the characteristics and linguistic profiles of the members of the Convention's Secretariat and Praesidium. This does not mean, however, that the French version of the Convention's text is always superior. For example, the Italian version is often more elegant and the German version is at times more precise.

That may prompt the question: which text is the one to read? This raises an important issue, particularly since the text will obviously be read more often in English than in other languages. Moreover, many of the official translations of the Convention's text took the English version as a point of departure. Nevertheless, it would be a mistake to regard the English version of the Convention's text as particularly authoritative. Indeed, it was much less elegant and often less rigorous than its Italian, French and German counterparts. The lacklustre English translation of the Convention's text also partly explains the ruthless attacks by *The Economist*, which recommended tossing the text unceremoniously into the rubbish bin.

A few examples serve to illustrate the shortcomings of the English version of the Convention's text. First, Giscard d'Estaing and other Convention members who were non-native English speakers insisted emphatically that the European Council was to be headed by a *Chairman*, and not by a *President*. By referring to a *Chairman*, they wanted to emphasise that the post was ceremonial in nature, akin to the Italian President, for example, as opposed to a dominant political figure such as the current French President. However, the title *Chairman* in English is somewhat inelegant, and inappropriately calls to mind rather a Board of Directors running a company instead of the presiding figure overseeing the work of a Union of 25 countries. There was also the option of *Chair of the European Council*, but this sounded too much like a piece of furniture. *Chairman* was too masculine and hence politically incorrect, but the unwieldy term *Chairperson* was hardly a better alternative. To make things more confusing, although the relevant disposition (Article 21 of the Convention's text) was entitled *The European Council Chair*, it actually provided that "[t]he European Council shall elect its *President* . . ." (emphasis supplied). But what made the English text especially odd was that it deviated from the French and Italian versions (*Président* and *Presidente*, respectively) as well as the German version, which indeed uses the term *Präsident* despite the fact that *Vorsitzender* – which conveys the ideas of both "chair" and "priority" – would have been etymologically consistent with the Latin *presiedere*. Common sense won out in the end, and the IGC changed the title of the provision – now Article I-22 of the Constitution – to *The European Council President*.

However, even the IGC's final English version of Article I-22 should be handled with care. According to this provision, the President "shall chair" the European Council "and drive forward its work". This is a clear example where one may draw different conclusions depending on which version of the text is consulted. The expression "drive forward" seems relatively dynamic in comparison with the French *anime* and the Italian *anima*. *Animer* and *animare* translate loosely as "to liven up" or "to stimulate", which would seem to suggest a role somewhat different from that of a President that "drives forward" an organisation's work. Meanwhile, the German *leitet* – "to steer" – evokes yet a third possible meaning. Considering the rather contentious debates surrounding the proposal of a full-time President of the European Council, it is easy to see that these questions of interpretation are not merely matters of style.

But while some translation errors lead to bemusement, obscurity, or just plain irritation, others can create serious problems of interpretation with substantive consequences. Despite the best intentions of the Convention, which strove to avoid resorting to the usual trick of using ambiguous language to expedite compromises, a problem arose in connection with Article 28 of the Convention's text (*The Court of Justice*), where the various translations diverged significantly. Article 28 articulated the principle (established by the Court of Justice and enshrined in Article II-47 of the Convention's text – now Article II-107 of the Constitution), according to which EU citizens are entitled to effective legal protection. In contrast to the French and German versions, the English and Italian versions appeared to introduce a distinction between two kinds of legal norms. The English text, in particular, was utterly deficient. According to this version, "Member States shall provide *rights of appeal* sufficient to ensure effective legal protection in the field of Union law." (emphasis supplied) However, the expression "rights of appeal" fails to convey the essential idea that a citizen may bring his or her case before a *court of law*, and that administrative appeals are insufficient. The legal experts had failed to catch this error by the time the Constitution was adopted in June of 2004, and it was not until August of that year that the problem was resolved. Article 28 of the Convention's text became Article I-29 of the Constitution, which provides that "Member States shall provide *remedies* sufficient to ensure effective legal protection in the fields covered by Union law." (emphasis supplied)

Finally and unfortunately, an opportunity was missed to improve certain deficiencies in the English-version provisions carried over from the Treaty of Rome, which was adopted in conjunction with the UK's accession to the Community in 1973. To cite but one example, the French version of the original Article 222 (now

Article 295) of the Treaty of Rome states: "*Le présent traité ne préjuge en rien le régime de la propriété dans les États membres.*" This provision can be translated rather literally into English as "The present Treaty shall in no way prejudice the system of property of the Member States." However, the official English translation reads: "This Treaty shall in no way prejudice *the rules in Member States governing the system of property ownership.*" (emphasis supplied) This odd formulation has led to some significant misconceptions about the nature and purpose of this provision. For example, it has been understood by some commentators as having a prophylactic influence on efforts to harmonise the property laws of the Member States. However, Article 222 of the Treaty of Rome was by no means intended to have an impact on the rules comprising the property laws of the Member States. To the contrary, the provision functioned as a guarantee to the Member States that they were free to establish and maintain the property *system* of their choice, i.e., a system of either public or private ownership, or both. In particular, Article 222 guaranteed that Member States were free to nationalise and/or privatise industries (e.g., in the transport, energy and telecommunications sectors) as they saw fit, without interference from the Community. Yet this provision, which has become Article III-425, and other poor translations of the original provisions of the Treaty of Rome remain untouched (other than the fact that the word "Treaty" has been replaced by "Constitution").

Notwithstanding the foregoing remarks, overall the lawyer-linguists of the Council did a commendable job in preparing the various translations of the Constitution. Their intense work during the summer of 2004 also explains why the final text was not signed until later that year on the 29th of October.

Criticism is easy, art is difficult. In a valiant effort to secure the highest linguistic and stylistic purity for the Convention's text, Giscard d'Estaing, shortly before the conclusion of the Convention's work, proposed to submit the entire text to the *Académie française* and "to the Academies of the other countries". And indeed, the *Académie française* did review the style and grammar of Part I of the French version of the Convention's text. However, as for the other versions, despite Giscard's good intentions, the problem is that there *is* no equivalent to the *Académie française* in most of the other Member States. The responsibility for making the necessary refinements to the various texts thus fell to the IGC. The modifications made, from the first drafts presented by the Convention in 2003 to the final text signed on 29 October 2004, demonstrate that many of the criticisms that had been aimed at the first texts were heard and acted upon. As such criticisms may no longer be valid, detractors should of course verify whether the deficiencies persist in the text (and in its 21 translations) before denouncing them.

CHAPTER III

THE EUROPEAN CONVENTION: A CONSTITUTION IS BORN

1. FROM A "BODY" TO A CONVENTION

"To bury a problem, one need only commission a study", as the French statist and Prime Minister Georges Clémenceau would have said. This philosophy has been applied more than once by the leaders of the Member States, above all when meeting in the European Council. Indeed, the published reports written by expert commissions (or by "Wise Men") for the purpose of lighting the way toward further European integration have been numerous and sundry. To cite but a few, these include the Davignon Report of 1970; the Vedel Report of 1972; the Tindemans Report of 1975; the London Report of 1981; the Dooge Report of 1985; and the Report of the Three Wise Men (Jean-Luc Dehaene, Richard von Weizsäcker and David Simon) of 1999.

Among the proposals contained in these reports, some have been taken up here and there by the various Intergovernmental Conferences (IGCs), but for the most part these reports lie dormant in archives, or have been published only in volumes of texts frequented only by intrepid students. The work of the Convention deserves more careful handling and will not be so easily forgotten.

In describing the composition of the group that was to be responsible for drafting the Charter of Fundamental Rights, the tone of the European Council meeting in Cologne on the 3rd and 4th of June, 1999 betrayed a total absence of enthusiasm for the project. Indeed, the relevant working group did not even think of a specific name for the assembly, and simply referred to a "*body* composed of . . . ".

European Council Decision on the Drawing Up of a Charter of Fundamental Rights of the European Union (excerpt from Annex IV of the Presidency Conclusions from the Cologne European Council of 3-4 June 1999)

In the view of the European Council, a draft of such a Charter of Fundamental Rights of the European Union should be elaborated by a body composed of representatives of the Heads of State and Government and of the President of the Commission as well as of members of the European Parliament and national parliaments. Representatives of the European Court of Justice should participate as observers. Representatives of the Economic and Social Committee, the Committee of the Regions and social groups as well as experts should be invited to give their views. Secretariat services should be provided by the General Secretariat of the Council.

*European Council Decision on the Drawing Up of a Charter of Fundamental Rights
of the European Union (excerpt from Annex IV of the Presidency Conclusions from
the Cologne European Council of 3-4 June 1999)* (Cont'd)

This body should present a draft document in advance of the European Council in December 2000. The European Council will propose to the European Parliament and the Commission that, together with the Council, they should solemnly proclaim on the basis of the draft document a European Charter of Fundamental Rights. It will then have to be considered whether and, if so, how the Charter should be integrated into the treaties.

However, from the very first meeting of this "body" in December of 1999, the members of the group decided to refer to themselves as a *Convention* – and the implicit suggestion of a constitutional process, i.e., a constitutive process, was obvious. For example, the Germans in the group, including in particular its President, Roman Herzog (who had previously been a President of Germany, a Judge of the Federal Constitutional Court of Karslruhe and a professor of constitutional law) could not help but think of the *Verfassungskonvent* ("Constitutional Convention") of Herrenchiemsee in 1948. The French members, meanwhile, recalled the Convention that proclaimed the French Republic during its first meeting on 21 September 1792.

In May of 1787, the representatives of the 13 former British colonies in America – with the exception of Rhode Island – gathered in Philadelphia in what was probably the most famous constitutional assembly in history. According to their mandate, these representatives were to present and consider proposals for amendments to certain provisions of the treaties which united those 13 states, i.e., the Articles of Confederation. However, proceeding under the Presidency of the delegate from the state of Virginia, George Washington, the assembly adopted an agenda that envisaged "the institution of a national government, endowed with legislative, executive and judicial branches". There can be little doubt that the *body* conceived in Cologne in 1999 also had the American Constitutional Convention in the forefront of its mind.

Having shown its audacity by naming itself a *Convention*, the members of the *body* worked diligently and adopted a text on 2 October 2000. Two weeks later in Biarritz, France, the text was unanimously accepted by the European Council. This consensus was not easily achieved, however, owing above all to the inclusion in the Charter of numerous social rights which clashed with the sensibilities of certain Member States.

Despite the hard-won unanimous adoption of the Charter by the European Council, the views of commentators writing about the Charter were very much divided, especially among jurists. However, the text is a *tour de force*, setting forth in a relatively clear manner many principles culled from the foundational Treaties, Community regulations and directives, numerous decisions of the Court of Justice, and the European Convention of Human Rights as interpreted by the European Court of Human Rights in Strasbourg.

With the right mix of audacity and political realism, the 62 members of this first Convention (supplemented by nearly as many alternates and 12 observers) made believers of many sceptics, including politicians, professors and specialists in European affairs, and demonstrated to them that the formula of the Convention was valid. This success was largely due to the combination of technical acumen – including the legal expertise necessary for the drafting of the text – and the readability of the final result.

Furthermore, the first Convention was sufficiently representative of all the institutions at both the European and national levels to have as much legitimacy, if not more, than the traditional Intergovernmental Conferences. This plainly distinguished the Convention from all of the committees of "wise men" that had preceded it. Another point of distinction is that, although certain compromises were unavoidable, the Convention was not subject to the kind of diplomatic bartering and corridor agreements that have always characterised the IGCs. These advantages of the Convention explain why, ever since 1999, the proposals for reforming the Treaty revision procedures have all made reference to the Convention model.

2. The Laeken Mandate: The Convention on the Future of Europe

There is such a clear continuity between the Convention of 1999-2000, which was responsible for the Charter, and the European Convention of 2002-2003, that it is easy to underestimate the effort made throughout the year in 2001 to secure the adoption of the Convention formula by the Member States at the Laeken summit of 14-15 December. Credit for this successful effort is unquestionably due to Belgian Prime Minister Guy Verhofstadt, who presided at the summit. In the days immediately following the Nice summit in December of 2000, Verhofstadt was already taking steps in anticipation of the summit to be held the following year, with the help of several key figures including: his predecessor, Jean-Luc Dehaene; Italian Prime Minister Giuliano Amato; former Commission President Jacques Delors; former Polish Foreign Minister Borislaw Geremek; and David Miliband, a close collaborator of British Prime Minister Tony Blair, who was later elected to the British Parliament.

At Nice, the heads of State and government had adopted a Treaty that was supposed to resolve the institutional problems linked to enlargement, which had been left unresolved since the time of the Maastricht Treaty. However, the Treaty was adopted by a group traumatised by the horse-trading and deal-making that kept the negotiators at the table long into the final night of work. This is clear from the "Declaration on the future of the Union", annexed to the Treaty of Nice, and especially from the unenthusiastic opening line of point 1: "Important reforms have been decided in Nice."

There is no reference to a *Convention* in the Nice Declaration, although a "deeper and wider debate" is envisaged at point 3. However, between Nice and Laeken, there was not only the perseverance of those who had for some time advocated a decisive step toward political union but also an unexpected wakeup call: the Irish referendum of 7 June 2001. To the astonishment of those – and there were many– who had forgotten the warning shots fired in Denmark and France in 1992, or who had failed to understand them, the Irish voters, by a margin of 53.88% to 46.12%, refused to authorise their government to ratify the Treaty of Nice. Without realising it, the Irish were strengthening the hand of those who considered it unthinkable (especially following the Nice experience) to continue reforming the Union solely by means of the IGC.

Declaration on the Future of the Union

1. Important reforms have been decided in Nice. The Conference welcomes the successful conclusion of the Conference of Representatives of the Governments of the Member States and commits the Member States to pursue the early and successful ratification of the Treaty of Nice.

2. It agrees that the conclusion of the Conference of Representatives of the Governments of the Member States opens the way for enlargement of the European Union and underlines that, with ratification of the Nice Treaty, the European Union will have completed the institutional changes necessary for the accession of new Member States.

3. Having opened the way to enlargement, the Conference calls for a deeper and wider debate about the future development of the European Union. In 2001, the Swedish and Belgian Presidencies, in cooperation with the Commission and involving the European Parliament, will encourage wide-ranging discussions with all interested parties; representatives of national Parliaments and all those reflecting public opinion; political, economic and university circles, representatives of civil society, etc. The candidate States will be associated with this process in ways to be defined.

4. Following a report to Göteborg in June 2001, the European Council, at its meeting at Laeken/Brussels in December 2001, will agree on a declaration containing appropriate initiatives for the continuation of this process.

5. The process should address, *inter alia*, the following questions:
– how to establish and monitor a more precise delimitation of competencies between the European Union and the Member States, reflecting the principle of subsidiarity;
– the status of the Charter of Fundamental Rights of the European Union proclaimed in Nice, in accordance with the conclusions of the European Council in Cologne;
– a simplification of the Treaties with a view to making them clearer and better understood without changing their meaning;
– the role of national Parliaments in the European architecture.

6. Addressing the above-mentioned issues, the Conference recognises the need to improve and to monitor the democratic legitimacy and transparency of the Union and its institutions, to bring them closer to the citizens of the Member States.

7. After these preparatory steps, the Conference agrees that a new Conference of the Representatives of the Governments of the Member States will be convened in 2004, to treat the above-mentioned items in view of the related Treaty changes.

---

8. The Conference of Member States shall not constitute any form of obstacle or precondition to the enlargement process. Moreover, those candidate States which have concluded accession negotiations with the Union shall be invited to participate in the Conference. Those candidate States which have not concluded their accession negotiations shall be invited as observers.

Showing subtle diplomatic skill, the Belgian Prime Minister succeeded in convincing his counterparts, and by the time of the Laeken summit, the idea of establishing a new Convention was already taken for granted. Furthermore, the essential content of the Convention's mandate was already clear. It would be expected to develop point 5 of the Nice Declaration, which referred to delimitation of competences, the "status" of the Charter, simplification of the Treaties, and the role of national parliaments. The discussions at Laeken focused on the Convention's Presidency. Who would preside? Would he or they be regarded as representatives of their Member State of origin? How many members would compose the Praesidium? Etc.

Laeken Declaration (excerpt)

III. Convening of a Convention on the Future of Europe

In order to pave the way for the next Intergovernmental Conference as broadly and openly as possible, the European Council has decided to convene a Convention composed of the main parties involved in the debate on the future of the Union. In the light of the foregoing, it will be the task of that Convention to consider the key issues arising for the Union's future development and try to identify the various possible responses.

The European Council has appointed Mr V. Giscard d'Estaing as Chairman of the Convention and Mr G. Amato and Mr J.L. Dehaene as Vice-Chairmen.

Composition

In addition to its Chairman and Vice-Chairmen, the Convention will be composed of 15 representatives of the Heads of State or Government of the Member States (one from each Member State), 30 members of national parliaments (two from each Member State), 16 members of the European Parliament and two Commission representatives. The accession candidate countries will be fully involved in the Convention's proceedings. They will be represented in the same way as the current Member States (one government representative and two national parliament members) and will be able to take part in the proceedings without, however, being able to prevent any consensus which may emerge among the Member States.

[. . .]

Length of proceedings

The Convention will hold its inaugural meeting on 1 March 2002, when it will appoint its Praesidium and adopt its rules of procedure. Proceedings will be completed after a year, that is to say in time for the Chairman of the Convention to present its outcome to the European Council.

Working methods

The Chairman will pave the way for the opening of the Convention's proceedings by drawing conclusions from the public debate. The Praesidium will serve to lend impetus and will provide the Convention with an initial working basis.

Laeken Declaration (excerpt) (Cont'd)

[...]

Final document

The Convention will consider the various issues. It will draw up a final document which may comprise either different options, indicating the degree of support which they received, or recommendations if consensus is achieved.

Together with the outcome of national debates on the future of the Union, the final document will provide a starting point for discussions in the Intergovernmental Conference, which will take the ultimate decisions.

Forum

In order for the debate to be broadly based and involve all citizens, a Forum will be opened for organisations representing civil society (the social partners, the business world, non-governmental organisations, academia, etc.). It will take the form of a structured network of organisations receiving regular information on the Convention's proceedings.

[...]

Secretariat

The Praesidium will be assisted by a Convention Secretariat, to be provided by the General Secretariat of the Council, which may incorporate Commission and European Parliament experts.

Reading with hindsight, the Laeken mandate shows the extent to which the members of the Convention were able to capitalise on the *marges de manoeuvre* they were given. However, it was essential for the Convention to respect its mandate in order not to give any pretext to the most sceptical governments, who willingly would have filed away the "final document" if they could have done so. This explains why Giscard d'Estaing insisted on presenting at least the first two parts of the Convention's text at the Thessaloniki summit of 20 June 2003 instead of waiting until after the summer, as many members of the Convention had urged.

The composition of the Convention and the time allotted to it had been fixed from the outside; it was up to the members themselves, however, to decide on a name. The term "European Convention" was chosen (with a subtle change in meaning compared to the "Convention on the future of Europe" of the Laeken Declaration), thus transforming a series of meetings into a veritable – albeit temporary – institution.

The Convention's ability to capitalise on its mandate is manifest in particular in its final product. It had not been easy to introduce the term "Constitution" in the Laeken Declaration. During the press conference at the close of the Laeken summit, certain differences of opinion became evident, for example between German Chancellor Gerhard Schröder – who called for a "Constitution worthy of such a name" – and British Prime Minister Tony Blair, who stated, "despite such ambitions, Europe is moving forward more pragmatically under the influence of France and the United Kingdom in particular".

In December of 2001, the European Council charged the Convention with preparing "a final document which may comprise either different options, indicating the degree of support which they received, or recommendations if consensus is achieved". In July of 2003, the Council received a single text bearing the title of "Constitution" and offering only one *option*: to move Article IV-1, the provision concerning the symbols of the Union, to Part I of the text.

When considered in the light of the Laeken mandate, Giscard's "*imparfaite mais inespérée*" takes on its full meaning. To appreciate the sense of *inespérée* ("beyond what could be hoped for"), one need only think of the diversity of visions and interests held by the 105 members of the Convention, their alternates, the institutions that nominated them (and to whom they had to report), and their professional entourages, both within and outside the halls of the European Parliament in Brussels, where the Convention met at least twice a month from 28 February 2002 to 10 July 2003.

3. A Melting Pot of Divergent Visions and Interests

The composition of the Convention defies simplistic descriptions: there were numerous fractures and ruptures that had to be overcome before the first two parts of the text were adopted in the plenary session of 10 June 2003 and before the remainder of the text was delivered to the President of the European Council on 18 July of that year. During the preceding IGCs in which significant reforms to the Treaties had been made, each of the 12 – and then 15 – of the participating governments had simultaneously defended its own essential interests and the European policy interests that had already by and large been long established and thus easy to identify. In the Convention, things were more complicated. To understand the debates that influenced the Convention and shaped its text, it is necessary to keep in mind at least four distinct perspectives, i.e., four different orientations regarding what the Union should be and where it should be going.

3.1. Four Visions of Europe

The ideological positions regarding European integration may be grouped into four categories which, little by little, have been crystallising within the context of the continuing debate on Europe. These four visions of Europe are: *federalist, functionalist, intergovernmentalist* and *nationalist* (or *souverainiste*, as the French say).

The *federalist* vision of Europe is typically associated with the name of Altiero Spinelli (1907-1986). This approach can be summarised – when it is not being caricaturised – in two points. First, the *objective* is to create a European federation endowed with external sovereignty, comparable in certain respects to the United States. Second, the *means* consists of federal institutions, established by a

Constitution, including most importantly a Parliament that represents the peoples of Europe. A federal Europe would thus fundamentally be linked to democratic institutions.

Interest in the federalist vision, which was for a long time considered utopian and which in practice was eclipsed by the more pragmatic approach of Jean Monnet, re-emerged dramatically in 1992 in connection with the ratification of the Treaty of Maastricht. This was due in large part to the fact that the prevailing, excessively technocratic approach to European integration was identified as the root cause of the "no" vote in Denmark in the referendum of 2 June 1992, and of the hesitant acceptance by the French in the referendum of 20 September.

At present it is not easy to say with certainty who the real supporters of the federalist view are, since the members of the Convention and the various commentators did not fail to extol the virtues of democracy and political union, whatever their true convictions regarding European integration may have been. However, the construction of a federal Europe is perhaps most eloquently articulated in the contributions made by Andrew Duff, Member of the European Parliament for the East of England and chair of the Liberal caucus during the Convention. All of the elements in the Constitution that promote the protection of rights and the democratic character of the Institutions may be said, in some sense, to be linked to the federalist cause.

The *functionalist* perspective is forever linked to the name of Jean Monnet (1888-1979) and is found at the very heart of the Treaty of Paris of 1951, which established the *Community method* (see pages 21–24). Much more pragmatic than the federalist approach, although they share common aspirations, the functionalist approach insists more on the *method* than on the objective. This method is linked closely to the Institutions created to drive forward European integration, which were conceived above all as a means to overcome the national self-interest that biases the positions of the diplomatic services.

On this view, the solidarity and fusion of interests achieved progressively in fields of ever-widening scope will lead, little by little, to a transfer of powers from the traditional sovereign State to the common Institutions. The preparation by an independent Commission of proposals to be approved by a qualified majority of the Council of Ministers represents the "motor" of integration. The continuous generation and refinement of proposals which in turn necessitate new ones is the "fuel". Meanwhile, the success of the "Common Market" will entice more European States to join the Community; the realisation of a single market will require a single currency; a single currency will entail economic governance; economic governance will call for a Constitution; and so on.

The functionalist approach is doubly exposed to the risks of technocracy. This is due first of all to the particularity of the Institutions, including the Commission, whose members are not democratically elected. Second, adherents of this approach seek to avoid revealing too quickly the consequences of each stage of integration, for fear of offending the sensitivities of the Member State governments attached to their national sovereignty. Jacques Delors, who was President of the Commission from 1985 to 1995, was perhaps the last of the true believers in the functionalist method who knew how to effectively communicate a vision of European integration.

During the proceedings of the Convention, the clearest expression of the functionalist perspective was undoubtedly the *Penelope* document, i.e., the "feasibility study" of a Constitutional Treaty produced at the request of Commission President Romano Prodi by his staff and presented as a contribution to the Convention by the Commission's two representatives, Michel Barnier and Antonio Vitorino.

The *intergovernmentalist* vision was for a long time associated with Charles de Gaulle (1890-1970) and with his slogan of "*l'Europe des patries*" ("Europe of motherlands"). This approach is generally perceived as being hostile to European integration, as it represents the defiant preservation of national sovereignty. Its roots are as old as European intergovernmental cooperation itself, first manifest in the Vienna Congress of 1814-15. De Gaulle held in contempt everything Monnet stood for and opposed him at every turn. The Fouchet Plans of October 1961 and of January 1962, whereby de Gaulle sought to re-launch the political construction of Europe in 1964, openly rejected the Community method.

The intergovernmentalist approach is characterised by the objective of reinforcing interstate cooperation propelled by the most important countries. The key Institution is therefore the European Council. De Gaulle would have been astounded (or indeed apoplectic!) if he could have read the enthusiastic pages devoted to that Institution in Monnet's *mémoires* following its establishment in 1972.

Intergovernmental cooperation was for a long time applied principally in those areas which are strictly political: external policy, security and defence. Then, beginning with the Treaty of Maastricht, intergovernmentalism was given new and unexpected support by the German *Länder* and by other regions with legislative powers, in particular in Belgium and Spain, who deemed it unacceptable that their respective governments could take decisions in the Council of Ministers affecting the spheres of influence guaranteed to them by their national constitutions.

Finally, the intergovenmentalist approach was further boosted by the work of the European Council of Lisbon in March of 2000 thanks to a growing interest in the so-called *open method of coordination* as a new means to pursue a *rapprochement* of national social and employment policies. Crudely put, the open method of coordination is a kind of benchmarking used in areas which, without being directly linked to national sovereignty, are nevertheless politically sensitive and closely conditioned on the agendas of political parties at the national level.

During the Convention it was evident that many of the delegates suspected Giscard d'Estaing of being a champion of the classic intergovernmentalist approach and a natural representative of the interests of the largest Member States. However, those who feared his possible allegiance to the intergovernmentalist camp had forgotten that Giscard, despite his instrumental role in creating the European Council, also contributed actively to the establishment of both the election by universal suffrage of the European Parliament (plainly a *federalist* initiative) and the European Monetary System (a *functionalist* project and forerunner to the single currency).

Yet while *Giscard* is clearly not de Gaulle's heir in matters of European integration, it emerged in 2003 that British Prime Minister Tony Blair – represented at the Convention by Peter Hain – clearly is. Like de Gaulle, Blair's vision of European integration blends a strong sense of pragmatism with the goal of a Europe guided by the leadership of the oldest and largest Member States. As for the other governments participating at the Convention, it is difficult to know to what extent they were attached to the intergovernmentalist agenda. Each time a government showed hostility toward extending qualified majority voting to certain policy areas, or whenever the most egalitarian representation of the Member States was favoured, such positions could possibly have reflected the desire to defend certain national or policy-specific interests.

The *nationalist* vision is clearly linked to the hostile reactions to the Maastricht Treaty in certain Member States. Two characteristics distinguish this perspective from the intergovernmentalist approach. First, there is an insistence on matters of principle, which may be contrasted with the relative pragmatism of both de Gaulle and Blair. Second, and more importantly, exponents of the nationalist view lack any kind of structured programme for Europe.

Furthermore, the nationalist perspective may be distinguished in that the federalist, functionalist and intergovernmentalist approaches to European integration are all in reality largely complementary. This can be seen from the fact that, since its inception the Union has made substantial albeit non-linear strides under the more or less contemporaneous influence of all three visions. The *projet souverainiste* (i.e., the nationalist approach) is fundamentally incompatible with those perspectives and regards European cooperation as a *zero sum game*, to borrow the oft-used jargon of game theory. In a *positive* sum game, every player wins and takes a share of the pooled resources of all the players whereas, in a zero sum game, the winnings are proportional to the resources at stake. Since the "size of the pie" is fixed, if a player wins, his payoff is necessarily to the detriment of another. Compared with the other visions of European integration, the nationalist view is paradoxically more optimistic with respect to the problem-solving capacity of States, because it negates the fundamental risk of the divergent interests in Europe being pitted against each other.

The Convention of 2002-03 differed radically from the ICGs that preceded it in that, for the first time, those espousing the nationalist vision were given a forum to express their views openly. Evidence of this camp's active use of the Convention can be seen in the systematic interventions of Jens-Peter Bonde, David Heathcoat-Amory and William Abitol, as well as in the alternative draft Constitution entitled "One voice for millions of people", signed by seven members of the Convention and twelve parliamentarians from various Member States and candidate countries. However, it was obvious during the debates in plenary that, by railing against the advance of Europe, the nationalists succeeded mostly in bringing the adherents of the other three camps closer together.

3.2. Openly Declared Political Allegiances

The Convention method made it possible to see, more clearly than any IGC had before it, the alignments of the participants according to the various political parties active in Europe. The interaction of political parties has seldom had any influence on European integration, and one of the ironies of history is that the Franco-German axis, which has long been a source of some of the most important European reforms, was particularly effective when the Liberal Giscard d'Estaing cooperated with the Social Democrat Schmidt, and when Mitterand, a Socialist, cooperated with the Christian Democrat Kohl.

The most influential political parties represented in the European Parliament certainly do not oppose each other on the concept of an integrated Europe as such. Indeed, these parties include among their ranks supporters of all the various approaches to European integration discussed in the preceding section. This is apparent, for example, in the case of the European People's Party (EPP), the European Socialist Party (PES) and the Liberal Democrats (ELDR), i.e., the three grand battalions of the

Political Alignments at the Convention

Parties		Members	Alternates	Praesidium
EPP-DE	61	Presidency 2		*Pres. 2*
European People's Party –		Governments 6	Govts. 5	*Govts. 1*
European Democrats		National Parliaments 24	Nat. Parl. 16	*Nat Parl. 1*
(*centre right*)		European Parliament 6		
		Commission 1	Eur. Parl. 6	*Eur. Parl. 1*
		Observers 4		
				Comm. 1
			Obs. 2	
PES	58	Presidency 1		*Pres. 1*
European Socialist Party		Governments 5	Govts. 3	*Govts. 1*
(*centre left*)		National Parliaments 19	Nat. Parl. 15	*Nat. Parl. 2*

Political Alignments at the Convention (Cont'd)

Parties		Members	Alternates	Praesidium
		European Parliament 5 Commission 1 Observers 2	Eur. Parl. 5	*Eur. Parl. 1*
				Comm. 1
			Obs. 2	
ELDR Alliance of Liberals and Democrats for Europe (*centre – liberal tradition*)	17	Governments 4 National Parliaments 6 European Parliament 1 Observers 1	Govts. 1 Nat. Parl. 17 Eur. Parl. 1 Obs. 2	*Govts. 1*
UEN Union for Europe of Nations	9	Governments 2 European Parliament 1 National Parliaments 1	Govts. 1 Eur. Parl. 1 Nat. Parl. 3	
Greens-ALE Greens-European Free Alliance	8	Governments 1 European Parliament 1	Eur. Parl. 1 Nat. Parl. 4	
GUE-NGL Confederal Group of the European United Left - Nordic Green Left	5	National Parliaments 1 European Parliament 1	Nat. Parl. 2 Eur. Parl. 1	
EDD Group for a Europe of Democracies and Differences	2	European Parliament 1	Eur. Parl. 1	
Non-registered (*extreme right*)	3	National Parliaments 1	Nat. Parl. 1 Govts. 1	
No direct attachment to the parties of the European Parliament	45	Governments 9 National Parliaments 4 Observers 6	Govts. 17 Nat. Parl. 2 Comm. 2 Obs. 5	

Note: the numbers provided above are approximate and varied at different times. *Source*: Ries Baeten, *Who's Who in the Convention on the Future of the European Union*, brochure distributed at the Convention, edition of 5 February 2003.

Convention, as well as for some of the members of the Union for Europe of the Nations (UEN). The Greens/European Free Alliance are clearly sympathetic to the federalist cause, while the extreme left wing is more closely aligned with nationalism (and often linked to the anti-globalisation movement). Nationalism is openly embraced by Europe of Democracies and Differences but also has sympathisers in the UEN. The majority of the members of the Convention belonged to one of the foregoing political groupings of the European Parliament.

The last month of work during the Convention clearly showed the importance of these political parties, which served as important forums for developing mutually agreeable solutions. The links between Vice President Jean-Luc Dehaene and the Christian-Democratic party on the one hand, and between Vice President Giuliano Amato and the Socialists on the other, enabled Dehaene and Amato to function as catalysts for compromise between the two groups, with the support of the Liberals. The four major parties – the EPP, the Socialists, the Liberals and the Greens – were manifestly open to compromises which the more individualist logic of the IGC would not have permitted.

Of course, traditional political clashes were also apparent during the Convention, some of which may be seen in the compromises that surfaced in the text of the Constitution, particularly in the areas of "Social Europe" (comprising above all social and labour policy) and economic governance. In the case of Social Europe, these divisions did not preclude a compromise that entailed, on the one hand, the acceptance of the social rights contained in the Charter, and on the other hand, the abandonment of ambitions to reinforce the Community method in the social sphere. However, the price of such a compromise was the use of wording in the Constitution that was at times ambiguous and even contradictory. With respect to economic governance, the conservative positions of certain representatives, and a profound attachment to intergovernmentalism, explain the lack of any real progress toward the goal of a Council of Economic Ministers with clearly defined and reinforced powers.

3.3. The Representation of Well-Defined Interests

The ICGs have always been a marketplace where Member States can bargain and haggle with their national interests. A prime example of this is the recognition in both the Maastricht and Amsterdam Treaties of derogations in favour of Denmark and the United Kingdom. The dynamics of the Convention – in line with the hopes of its promoters – were quite different. On the other hand, national and institutional interests were present and could easily be detected.

It would be tedious here to list the national interests defended openly by the representatives of the various governments participating at the Convention (and more subtly by certain national and European parliamentarians). A complete inventory may be taken by carefully examining the contributions submitted during the proceedings, which are maintained on the Convention's website.

All of the governments represented naturally sought to promote their own interests – not only those of the fifteen Member States but also those of the ten countries that later joined the Union on 1 May 2004 and those of the countries still to join. However, the efforts of two delegations in particular proved spectacular. First, in the final weeks of the Convention there was the open opposition of the representative of the Spanish government, Alfonso Dastis, to the Presidency's plan to abandon the weighting of votes in the Council of Ministers. As a result of this clash, the Convention's text was altered so that, according to Article 24(3), the application of *double majority* voting (meaning, in relation to most policy areas, a majority of Member States representing three-fifths of the population of the Union) would not take effect until November of 2009, thus preserving the much-maligned Nice voting formula in the interim. The second case was the obstinacy of Peter Hain of the British government, who waged every possible campaign to thwart the introduction of the Charter into the Constitution. Hain's efforts led to the inclusion of the following bizarre sentence in the Preamble to the Charter: "In this context the Charter will be interpreted by the courts of the Union and the Member States with due regard to the explanations prepared under the authority of the Praesidium of the Convention which drafted the Charter and updated under the responsibility of the Praesidium of the European Convention." This addition to the Charter has been received with dismay by more than one commentator. However, it cannot prevent courts from having due regard for other interpretative elements.

In the two examples cited above, the final result is neither to the advantage of nor to the detriment of any Member State in particular. The Constitution does not contain any new provision specifically favouring the interests of any Member State, and indeed the modifications made to Part III contribute to the elimination of certain previously existing anomalies.

One of the great novelties of the Convention was the full participation of the representatives of the European Institutions. Although the Court of Justice and the European Central Bank did not have observer status – in contrast to certain consultative organs (i.e., the Economic and Social Committee and the Committee of the Regions) and the European Ombudsman – their Presidents were often heard in working groups and discussion circles.

In the ICGs of Amsterdam and Nice, the European Parliament was represented by two deputies, while the Commission has actively taken part in the preparatory work of the IGCs ever since the days of the Single European Act, signed in 1986. However, neither the Parliament nor the Commission had any institutional basis for their participation in the IGC itself, where decisions are taken solely upon the unanimous vote of the Member States. The alternative structure of the Convention allowed for a more open airing of the interests of all the Institutions – above all, those of the European Parliament, expressed emphatically indeed.

For its part, the Commission was relatively cautious in defending its own interests despite the committed involvement of Barnier and Vitorino, each of whom was a member of the Praesidium. The reason for this was the lack of cohesion in the college of Commissioners on the various issues examined by the Convention – at times because of the limited collegiality in the Prodi Commission, but most often due to profound divisions among the Commissioners with regard to the very objective of the Convention. Already prior to the summer of 2002, the Commission had officially presented a draft text to the Convention; yet the *Penelope* text referred to above, which was published on the 4th of December of that year, did not bear the Commission's name. Instead, the title page of this document states: "Feasibility study: Contribution to a preliminary draft – Constitution of the European Union – Working document". This document was produced, at the request of President PRODI in agreement with Mr BARNIER and Mr VITORINO by a working party [. . .]". The limited impact of the *Penelope* document may undoubtedly be explained in part by the fact that it did not appear to be the text of a united Institution.

The European Parliament advanced its own cause in a much more brazen manner, and its interests were defended by its representatives with determination – including against national parliaments, where the need arose. This could be seen particularly in the systematic opposition of the representatives of the Parliament to the idea of a "Congress of the peoples of Europe", favoured by Giscard d'Estaing. Giscard had indicated that he was very attached to this innovation. However, he relinquished this fond desire when the Presidency badly needed the support of the Parliamentarians against the intergovernmentalist reflex reactions of certain Member States in the days leading up to the session of 10 June 2003.

The Committee of the Regions was also active during the proceedings and was in the end supported by numerous members of the Convention at the session of 7 February 2003, when the role of regional and local authorities was discussed. The influence of the Committee of the Regions is evident in the provisions making reference to these authorities and the placement of the Committee of the Regions before the Economic and Social Committee in the list of consultative organs of the Union.

3.4. *"Old Europe" versus "New Europe" and the "Bigs" versus the "Smalls"*

The media paid relatively little attention to the proceedings of the Convention, except when they could play up the contrasts between the participants. Significantly, a large number of journalists pointed to the division between "old" and "new" Europe (to use the expressions infamously coined by US Secretary of Defence Donald Rumsfeld in January of 2003 to distinguish between cooperative countries and "problem" countries during the Iraq conflict) as the reason why the draft articles pertaining to the Institutions were the last to be presented and why these articles underwent several modifications. And when the press couldn't use the "new versus old" story, they harped on the opposing views of the large and small Member States.

This kind of sensationalist reporting at best reflects a disinterest in a process that could offer no spectacular announcements or, at worst, a lack of professionalism on the part of certain journalists from the general press. On the other hand, during the plenary sessions, the press box was always full, and the specialised international press agency *Agence Europe* gave a faithful account of all the developments in the Convention while also providing substantial commentary.

In fact, neither an attentive reading of the Constitution nor an in-depth study of the contributions made and the documents produced throughout the Convention reveal any significant division between old and new Europe. Of course, emotions ran high during the crisis of the war in Iraq. The differences between the countries led by the UK and Spain on the one hand and by France, Germany and Belgium on the other were clear to all, but these differences did not affect the work of the Convention. To the contrary, the members of the Convention and the shrewdest commentators pointed out that the crisis had actually served as a catalyst for the Convention's work – and indeed, overcoming adversity in this manner has become a rather common theme in the history of European integration. While it is true that decisions in the area of foreign policy and security remain subject to unanimity, the divisions between those countries favouring qualified majority voting and those clinging to unanimity do not correspond to the cleavages between old and new Europe or between the Bigs and the Smalls.

The differences between the large and small countries were more apparent insofar as they were referred to in plenary by many members of the Convention. However, in the final analysis, such references seem for the most part to have been nothing more than rhetoric, and in any event no alliances coalesced along any such clear lines. On many occasions, Convention members from countries of 15 million inhabitants or less adopted the same positions held by the so-called Bigs – and *vice versa*.

4. THE MEMBERS OF THE CONVENTION

The members of the Convention generally did not relish being called *convention-nels*, a term used avidly by Giscard d'Estaing to make a subtle distinction between the members of the Praesidium and the rest of the delegates. The final French version of the Convention's text contains a list of the participants broken down into three categories, *"Présidence – autres membres du Praesidium – conventionnels"*, whereas in the other linguistic versions only the comprehensive *"Members of the Convention"* appears. The reason for this is simple: the French noun *convention-nel* either does not readily translate into most of the other relevant languages or, worse still, it translates literally in some languages as an adjective with a rather pejorative ring. Furthermore, the *conventionnels* of 1791 did not have only successes to their credit: to say nothing of the Reign of Terror at the hands of

Robespierre's bloodthirsty *Comité de salut public* ("Committee of Public Safety"), it should also be recalled that the French Constitution of the Year III (1795), although it could boast of an excellent text, was suspended the very day it was to enter into force because the country was at war. As for the delegates gathering at a Convention in Philadelphia in the spring and summer of 1787, these individuals were anything *but* conventional!

As explained below, the members of the European Convention belonged to several categories that had been determined by the Laeken Declaration, according to criteria that are, in practice, of varying importance.

4.1. Four Components Characterising the Members of the Convention

The Convention was composed of members plucked from four types of institutions: national parliaments; national governments; the European Parliament; and the Commission. The general characteristics of these four kinds of delegates to the Convention may be described in the following manner.

First of all there were 56 representatives of the *national parliaments*, i.e., two from each of the 28 participating countries, plus an equal number of alternates. And if there was one aspect of the structure of the Convention that distinguished it from that of an ICG, it was the presence of these national parliamentarians. The fact that two members of parliament appeared from each country, which was necessary to respect the constitutional choices of certain countries that have bicameral systems, meant that, taking account of alternates, parliamentarians constituted the most numerous group in the Convention: 144 (i.e., 112 national parliamentarians plus 32 members of the European Parliament) out of a total of 207 official members.

The objective of those that had made the Convention a reality was to give life to a process that was more democratic than that of the IGCs by involving a large number of elected parliamentarians. As a result, the representatives of the national governments felt much more isolated when they took positions deviating from the majority, which clearly distinguishes the Convention from the ICG. Furthermore, the alternates of the national and European parliamentarians – who were also deputies, senators, etc., just as the official members – participated actively during the sessions, while the national governments were in general represented by only one person, either an official member or alternate.

The methods used for selecting national parliamentarians and for ensuring their accountability varied widely from country to country. In many cases, the designation of members and alternates was intended to reflect the balance between the majority and the opposition parties, or among the various political families. The French *Assemblée nationale* did not hesitate, however, to use the pretext of the elections of June 2002 to replace its official delegate – thus ensuring that the two delegates from the French Parliament both represented the majority party while the opposition was left only with alternate posts.

Some national parliamentarians worked intensively with their institutions of origin. They reported regularly to their peers at home and fed back their colleagues' observations to the Convention. For example, many contributions to the Convention were prepared by commissions working for the British House of Lords. By contrast, other representatives worked in a more isolated manner, reflecting a much more personal conception of their mandate.

The fact that the Convention's work was sometimes carried out without prominent publicity – which aroused persistent criticism – cannot be blamed on the working method used. Indeed, it was rather the responsibility of national parliaments and of the national media to rise to the challenge and ensure that the work in Brussels was closely followed. The only real fault that can be attributed to the Convention is that its timetable was so condensed that it didn't leave time for systematic and in-depth national debates on all of the important issues. Yet this timetable was imposed on the Convention both by the Laeken Declaration and by the Convention's working methods. In any event, the Convention can be credited with considerable progress when compared with the preceding IGCs, where most national governments were not obliged to report to their respective parliaments on the ongoing negotiations.

The second group of delegates consisted of 28 *government representatives*, i.e., one from each participating country, plus 28 alternates. The choice of the government representatives was very revealing with respect to the importance accorded to the Convention by each country. Certain governments from the beginning nominated their Foreign Minister (e.g., Louis Michel from Belgium and Hans van Mierlo from the Netherlands) or another important member of the government (Italian Deputy Prime Minister Gianfranco Fini) or someone close to the Prime Minister (Peter Hain of the UK). Other countries, by contrast, were content to take their time before making a definitive choice. In particular, the French and German governments stalled because national elections were scheduled to proceed two or three months after the Convention began its work. A certain number of individuals were thus nominated whose political clout was limited, although on the whole they had a very good knowledge of the dossiers.

The wind started blowing the other way when, at the beginning of November 2002, German Chancellor Gerhard Schröder picked Foreign Minister Joschka Fischer to replace Peter Glotz, a lesser-known Social Democrat and former member of the Bundestag. The German example was followed soon thereafter by French President Jacques Chirac, who replaced Socialist Pierre Moscovici, the ex-Minister for European Affairs, with Foreign Minister Dominique de Villepin. In the meantime, the Convention had accepted the conclusions of Working Group III, which recommended the explicit conferral of a single, consolidated legal personality on the Union. This was followed closely by the Convention's decision to proceed with the drafting of a constitutional treaty to supersede the Treaties of Rome and of Maastricht, and to abandon the three-pillar structure of the Union. Through their representatives, the participating national governments were able to present their proposals, such as the Franco-German proposal – the fruit of a Paris summit in January of 2003 – which was presented to the Convention in the form of a joint contribution by Fischer and de Villepin.

In the final months of the Convention, numerous members of the Convention and commentators complained that the Convention had been "infiltrated by the IGC". In other words, the familiar penchant for intergovernmental bargaining had crept into the scene at the margins of the Convention's proceedings. However, these negotiations should not be viewed as a blight on the Convention process; to the contrary, they are a mark of success, that is, a sign of the Convention's growing importance. Furthermore, if such negotiations had not occurred within the context of the Convention, it is doubtful that the Convention's work would have been given due weight by the IGC that followed in the summer of 2004.

The third group was composed of 16 *members of the European Parliament* and their alternates. As with the other groups, the role of the European Parliament in the Convention process was considerably different from its role in relation to the IGC. The Parliament had succeeded – although not without difficulty – in securing the participation of two of its members as observers at the IGCs leading to the Treaties of Amsterdam and of Nice. By comparison, at the Convention, the official members of the Parliament in fact outnumbered the delegates representing the governments of the Member States: 16 to 15. Thanks to the diligence of the Parliament's alternate representatives, the total number of the Parliament's delegates attending the plenary sessions often matched the number of representatives from all 28 participating governments.

The Parliament was represented at the Convention in a highly organised fashion. Led by Iñigo Méndez di Vigo, a member of the Praesidium, the delegates of the Parliament reflected the balance of political forces within that Institution. The delegation included members hailing from various countries, but it carefully avoided any systematic advocacy of national interests, which was not its role. Of all the groups represented, the Parliament can even take credit for having the most open attitude with respect to minority views, considering that, as noted earlier, outspoken eurosceptics numbered among its delegates.

The Parliament also closely followed the Convention's work. The Committee on Constitutional Affairs, in particular, produced numerous reports that played an important role in the overall orientations adopted by the Convention. This Committee also prepared – at the hands of *rapporteurs* Méndez di Vigo and Richard Corbett – the final report on the Constitution prior to its ratification by the Parliament in January of 2005.

Finally, two delegates representing the *Commission* (i.e., Michel Barnier and Antonio Vitorino) were present, each of whom was a Commissioner himself and worked as part of the Convention's Praesidium. The alternates sent by the Commission were high-ranking civil servants but they were not Commissioners and were not permitted to substitute in the Praesidium for their respective principals.

The Commission undoubtedly has less to gain from the Convention system than the European Parliament. However, although it has been customary for the Commission to be represented at the IGCs, it should be recalled that the Commission has no right to vote at the IGC, nor even a right – at least in a formal sense – to make proposals. The Commission had considerable influence in the preparation of the Single European Act in 1985 and of the Treaty of Maastricht in 1991. However, this was chiefly due to a very strong alliance between Commission President Jacques Delors, German Chancellor Helmut Kohl, and French President François Mitterand at a time when the Commissioners were united by a clear objective: the achievement of the internal market in the first instance, followed by the establishment of an economic and monetary union (EMU) and European citizenship.

Barnier (Commissioner for Regional Policy and Institutional Reform) and Vitorino (Commissioner for Justice and Home Affairs) were plainly selected to represent the Commission by virtue of their portfolios, but this was not the only reason. Barnier, who was charged with following the Convention's work on institutional reforms, had already participated as a Minister of the French government at the IGC of 1996-97 leading to the Treaty of Amsterdam, where he was involved, in particular, in the preparatory work of the Westendorp group. Meanwhile, Vitorino, whose task at the Convention was to work on freedom, security and justice as well as fundamental rights, had been a delegate to the Convention that prepared the Charter of Fundamental Rights in 1999-2000.

As alluded to previously, the twenty Commissioners had substantially divergent views as to what the objectives of the Convention were. Although Barnier and Vitorino can by no means be reproached for not faithfully representing the Commission's interests, their input at the Convention was a reflection not so much of the views of all the Commissioners serving from 1999-2004 but rather of the views of a more "abstract" Commission, as it were, embodying the functionalist approach to European integration.

Convention Delegates (and Alternates) from the Largest Member States

	France	Germany	Italy	United Kingdom
Presidency	V. Giscard d'Estaing	none	G. Amato	(J. Kerr, Secretary General)
National governments	P. Moscovici, followed by D. de	P. Glotz, followed by J. Fischer	G. Fini (F. Speroni)	P. Hain (Baroness P.

Convention Delegates (and Alternates) from the Largest Member States (Cont'd)

	France	Germany	Italy	United Kingdom
	Villepin P. Vimont, followed by P. Andréani)	(H.-M. Bury)		Scotland of Asthal)
National parliaments	A. Barrau, followed by P. Lequiller; H. Haenel (A.-M. Idrac, followed by J. Floch; R. Badinter)	J. Meyer; E. Teufel (P. Altmaier; W. Senff)	M. Follini; L. Dini (F.G. Basile; V.Spini)	D. Heathcoat-Amory; G. Stuart (Lord Maclennan of Rogart; Lord Tomlinson)
European Parliament	O. Duhamel; A. Lamassoure (W. Abitol; P. Bérès)	E. Brok; K. Hänsch; S.Y. Kaufmann (R. Rack; J. Würmeling)	C. Muscardini; A. Tajani (E. Paciotti)	A. Duff; T. Kirkhope; L. McAvan (N. McCormick; A. Earl of Stockton)
Commission	M. Barnier	none	none	none
Observers	Y. Cousquer, representing employers (CEEP); C. du Granrut, representing the Committee of the Regions; R. Briesch, representing the Economic and Social Committee	M. Dammeyer, representing the Committee of the Regions; G. Frerichs, representing the Economic and Social Committee	C. Martini, representing the Committee of the Regions; E. Gabaglio, representing employees (ETUC) (M. Sepi, representing the Economic and Social Committee)	none

4.2. The Praesidium

In addition to the other 102 members of the Convention and their alternates, the Convention was presided over by three individuals who were independent insofar as they did not represent any of the four groups discussed above but who had been nominated at the Laeken Summit to steer the course of the enterprise. These three were of course Giscard, Amato and Dehaene.

Valéry Giscard d'Estaing had realised, from the beginning of the autumn of 2001, that if he were to preside over a Convention that wrote the Union's first Constitution, he would secure himself a place forever in the pantheon of the "founding fathers" of Europe. Giscard spent his entire career in the centre-right political stream, and his commitment to the cause of Europe has never faltered. As a Minister of the French government led by Charles de Gaulle, Giscard was able to appreciate the limits of intergovernmentalism, but at the same time understood the importance of the personal involvement of leaders at the highest level. As President of the French Republic from 1974 to 1981, he contributed decisively to the project of economic and monetary integration, working with German Chancellor Helmut Schmidt to create the European Monetary System (i.e., a system designed to control inflation and stimulate growth by limiting the scope for exchange rate fluctuations among the participating currencies). During that time he also contributed to the reinforcement of political cooperation through the institutionalisation of the European Council. His defeat in the presidential election of 1981 clearly left some of his ambitions unfulfilled, but it also gave him the opportunity to get to know the European Institutions from the inside, as a member of the European Parliament from 1989 to 1993.

Both his detractors and supporters agree that, through his leadership style at the Convention, Giscard managed to irritate as much as seduce, uniting authoritarianism with humour: his parting gesture in the final plenary session was to feed some lettuce to the Chinese ceramic turtle Wukei, which he had placed on the dias at the end of the spring of 2002. Two other qualities for which he is well known are his brilliant mind and his capacity to manoeuvre. The manner in which he positioned himself, in anticipation of the Laeken summit, in order to secure the Presidency, presaged his ability to steer the work of the Convention to a successful finish.

Giuliano Amato, who had formerly served as Italian Prime Minister from 1992 to 1993 and from 2000 to 2001, was described following the Nice summit as a "dreamer" by President Chirac, according to the press. Amato had in fact reflected on and worked tenaciously on the European Constitution long before it entered Giscard's mind to preside over the Convention, and indeed, before the idea of the Convention was ever conceived. As professor of law at the European University Institute (EUI) in Florence, Amato had directed, in 1997-98, the first study – commissioned by the European Parliament – regarding the preparation of a draft "basic Treaty" that could be substituted for the Treaties of Rome and of Maastricht. Earlier, as Prime Minister in 1992-1993, he had paved the way for the decisive reforms necessary for Italy to qualify as a member of the Eurozone from its inception. Amato's experience and the work he carried out alongside his Belgian counterpart, Prime Minister Verhofstadt, made him the most authoritative candidate for the Presidency of the Convention.

A professor of constitutional law, a former head of the Italian competition law authority (the Autorità garante della concorrenza e del mercato), and a political figure called "Doctor Subtle" (*dottor sottile*) by the Italian press, Amato had both the precision of a jurist and the political ability necessary to co-manage the heterogeneous assembly that was the Convention and to ensure a text with the coherence worthy of a Constitution. His critical mind and his sly humour were evident during the plenary sessions over which he often presided, while his technical competence and ability to synthesise diverse viewpoints can be seen from the reports of the two working groups for which he was responsible (namely, those devoted to the legal personality of the Union and to simplification), which had a substantial impact on the final text.

Jean-Luc Dehaene, the champion of longevity as Belgian Prime Minister from 1992 to 1999, seemed to be the ideal candidate to succeed Delors as Commission President in 1995. However, his force of character, working capacity and commitment to Europe – which were evident at the time of the ratification of the Maastricht Treaty – could not be accepted by British Prime Minister John Major, whose position was seriously constrained by the eurosceptic wing of his Conservative Party. The nomination of Dehaene was thus vetoed by the UK, and the post of Commission President was filled instead by Luxembourgish Prime Minister Jacques Santer, who served in that capacity until the collective resignation of the Commission in 1999 under pressure from the European Parliament.

The vigour and tenacity of this Doctor in Laws are equalled only by his capacity for manoeuvre – an indispensable quality for managing the ministerial coalitions of a country where the linguistic differences (French, Dutch and German) are related, in highly complicated ways, to political and ideological divisions. In short, Dehaene's background provided him with the experience essential for guiding a body as complex as the Convention.

Dehaene had also for a long time been calling for a draft Treaty designed to lead to a *Europe of citizens*. As a member of the Committee of Wise Men charged with presenting proposals to the European Council at Nice, he had recommended that a feasibility study be carried out – for example, by the European University Institute – to determine how the Treaties could be reorganised and how their amendment procedures might possibly be simplified. In addition to conducting numerous plenary sessions, Dehaene's role at the Convention allowed him to demonstrate his ability to maintain contacts and find compromises, notably in the working group on external policy and the many meetings he organised with localities, regions and the associations representing civil society.

President Giscard and Vice Presidents Amato and Dehaene were joined by ten other members of the Praesidium that reflected all of the various groups taking part in the Convention. The Praesidium represented, however imperfectly, the balance between the various political forces and between the participating countries, although not all of the latter were represented. Thirteen was already a hefty number; had the group been any larger its effectiveness would not have been guaranteed.

The Members of the Praesidium

Member	Group	Nationality
Valéry Giscard d'Estaing	(President)	French
Giuliano Amato	(Vice President)	Italian
Jean-Luc Dehaene	(Vice President)	Belgian
Michel Barnier	Commission	French
John Bruton	National parliaments	Irish
Henning Christophersen	Govts: Danish Presidency	Danish
Klaus Hänsch	European Parliament	German
Giorgos Katiforis until February 2003;	Govts: Greek Presidency	Greek
Giorgos Papandréou from February 2003		
Iñigo Méndez di Vigo	European Parliament	Spanish
Ana Palacio until March 2003; Alfonso Dastis from March 2003	Govts: Spanish Presidency	Spanish
Alojz Peterle	Guest representing the candidate countries	Slovenian
Gisela Stuart	National parliaments	British
Antonio Vitorino	Commission	Portuguese

The lack of continuity in the representation of certain governments due to the rotation of the Presidency of the Union made the Praesidium's work particularly challenging. For example, in June of 2003, it was necessary to resort to the mediation of Ana Palacio to overcome an *impasse* created by Alfonso Dastis of Spain. This *impasse* arose when Dastis, reacting to the Praesidium's proposal of a new definition of qualified majority voting that would dispense with the complex system of weighted votes, refused to relinquish the voting advantage that Spain had secured at Nice.

It is also worth noting the gender bias of the Praesidium, considering that only two women served as members. While this is lamentable, the imbalance is of course not specific to the Praesidium but rather is reflective of a more general problem characterising the majority of European countries.

The role of the Praesidium was essential, as it was this group that made choices of principle and adopted the various draft texts submitted to the attention of the Convention. The Praesidium met prior to each plenary session and at least twice a month between such sessions, and then convened more or less constantly from the end of May until the beginning of June, 2003.

Many members of the Convention complained that they were repeatedly confronted with a *fait accompli*, i.e., that they didn't have sufficient input into the

Praesidium's decisions but merely had to accept them after the fact. For the representatives of the national parliaments and of the national governments, coordination with the Praesidium clearly was not easy, whereas those of the European Parliament and the Commission were already close to the action in Brussels and for that matter had recourse to familiar and well-worn procedures. In any event, their ultimate approval of the final text to rousing acclaim, and especially their manifest enthusiasm during the last two sessions, are perhaps a sign that the members of the Convention felt in the end that they had been heard.

4.3. The Observers: Just Like the Others?

Also participating at the Convention were delegates designated as *observers*. However, while these delegates did not have the rank of official members, the fact that the Convention never voted meant that, in practice, the difference between these two categories was of limited relevance. Indeed, the observers took part, just as the official members, in the plenary sessions and in the working groups, and received the same documents contemporaneously and through the same channels. The only perceptible difference was a light priority accorded by the Presidency to official members when giving speakers the floor.

The Committee of the Regions invested a great deal in the Convention, giving specific support to its six delegates and their alternates, who presented not only the global position of the Committee but also a series of individual contributions and amendments. The Committee also adopted a number of opinions elaborated specifically for the Convention, including an opinion, at the request of the European Parliament, on the role of the local and regional authorities of the Union.

The Economic and Social Committee (ECOSOC) had only three delegates and three alternates representing it at the Convention. This was because the "social partners" – i.e., employer associations and trade unions – which constitute two of the three main components of ECOSOC (along with other elements of "civil society"), were already represented by three observers.

Finally, The European Ombudsman, who had already participated at the Convention on the Charter of Fundamental Rights, was also invited as an observer. The Ombudsman's presence at the Convention was particularly justified: ever since 2001, he has played an important role in promoting respect for the Charter by the Institutions, as the fact that the Charter was only "proclaimed" and was not made binding does not prevent the Ombudsman from using it as a basis on which to evaluate claims of maladministration.

4.4. The All-Important Secretariat

If taken at face value, the Laeken Declaration could create the illusion of a great enthusiasm for the Convention on the part of the European Council. The fact is that, traditionally, although the "conclusions of the Presidency" and corresponding annexes do reflect the decisions of the European Council, their preparation is nevertheless the responsibility of the President currently in rotation. In the case of Laeken, the President of the Council was Belgian Prime Minister Verhofstadt, whose commitment to Europe was never in doubt.

Despite the openness of the Declaration to the idea of the Convention, however, when it came to giving the Convention financial resources, concerns clearly arose about limiting the independence and the role of the Convention as far as possible. Instead of authorising a budget that would permit the Convention to invite all the representatives of NGOs whose input it deemed useful, the European Council decided to have its Secretariat General provide the Convention with assistance. The Council further specified that experts from the Commission and from the European Parliament could also be detached for this purpose.

The advantage of the formula adopted was that the Secretariat of the Council already had the necessary expertise. However, the Council is of course the Institution that represents the Member States. Its decision to appoint its own Secretariat to support the Convention was both a reminder that the latter body was merely charged with giving an opinion to the future IGC and a sign that it was being watched.

The three members of the Presidency did their best to establish some autonomy. The public's attention was attracted by the financial aspects of the Convention due to unofficial requests by Giscard for a salary at the level of the President of the Commission, which were promptly withdrawn. Such a move may reflect Giscard's tactical ability as much as it does his taste for *grandeur*. The President marked the territory of the Convention, personally choosing the Secretary General, the British diplomat John Kerr, who had participated in the negotiations leading to the Treaty of Maastricht as permanent representative of the United Kingdom to the European Community. Amato and Dehaene also contributed to the selection of the personnel working in the Secretariat.

The Secretariat consisted of nineteen individuals plus the Secretary General, whose talents played an important role in the proceedings. In fact, the triumvirate presiding over the Convention was in reality – like the Three Musketeers of Alexandre Dumas – composed of *four* dashing swashbucklers: Giscard (Athos), Amato (Aramis) and Dehaene (Portos) could not have succeeded without the skilful assistance of Kerr (d'Artagnan – who incidentally becomes the Marshall of France during the siege of Maastricht . . .). The logistical support necessary for the meetings of the Convention was provided by the services of the European Council and the Parliament, whose premises in Brussels also served as the Convention's home. The staff seconded to the Convention had all the proficiency necessary to prepare the agenda, to formulate the turns of phrase, to draft the minutes of every session and to prepare a final general report.

The situation changed completely when it was time to draft the Constitution. Apart from the communications officer and Giscard's personal secretary, there were only fifteen drafters working alongside the assistant to the Secretary General (Annalisa Giannella, a civil servant of the European Council), all of whom were under constant pressure. They were the ones who, on the basis of the works of the Convention, drafted most of the first draft Articles. At the same time, they had to assist the working groups, providing them with explanatory notes and, where necessary, helping them to prepare final reports. Then they had to synthesise hundreds of contributions and thousands of amendments presented by the members of the Convention. To appreciate the immensity of their work, it has to be recalled that, since there was no discrimination between members and observers nor between principals and alternates, there were more than two hundred participants at the Convention who were producing, each day, documents that the Secretariat not only had to post on the internet but above all had to read and synthesise. Given these working conditions, it is clear that, notwithstanding the criticisms that may be directed against the general structure of the Convention's text or against the various formulations adopted, the quality and the coherence of the final result merit high praise.

5. NEITHER A PARLIAMENT NOR A CONFERENCE OF DIPLOMATS

The functioning of the Convention was unsettling for many politicians, civil servants, journalists and academics who are more accustomed to parliamentary proceedings or diplomatic conferences. The procedures, rhythm and working methods of the Convention did not correspond to either of those familiar fora, and indeed this led to errors of analysis on the part of more than one commentator as the work of the Convention progressed, and further led to unfounded criticisms of the final text.

The decision-making procedure based on consensus is not in itself mysterious, contrary to certain confused explanations that have been circulated on the subject. Indeed, every kind of assembly engages in consensus-building, at least unconsciously: the person presiding over the session presents a proposal and says, "No one is opposed?" – and the deal is done. The key is to convince any naysayers that they are in an absolute minority position and that they have nothing to gain by holding out, other than the satisfaction of a duel of honour. Of course, this kind of cajoling can only be effective if a large majority of the assembly is content with the compromise on which the proposal is based.

A procedure based on consensus thus requires lengthy preparation, as the Three Musketeers of the Convention undoubtedly realised. Giscard, Amato and Dehaene were also surely wary of the trap laid by the Laeken Declaration: "a final document which may comprise either different options, indicating the degree of support which they received, or recommendations if consensus is achieved". It would have been easy and expeditious to have the Convention vote on the Constitution on the basis of several candidate texts. The final report would have indicated the number of votes for and against each of the alternatives, possibly broken down by political affiliation or by country. However, this would have been a perfect way to ensure that only unanimously accepted proposals would be considered by the ICG. Instead of motivating the governments to make concessions, the requirement of transparency as enunciated in the Laeken Declaration would have pressured them to hunker down around their own positions, as the final text would have been the measure of their tenacity in defending their national interests.

Amato had participated in the difficult negotiations at the summit in Nice. Responding to the question of what made the Convention different from the IGC, he often explained that, in an IGC, "the Sovereign is heard to speak". In other words, government representatives present their positions without specifying the reasons for them, as a sovereign State need not justify itself. By contrast, in the Convention, and above all in the Praesidium, both government representatives and other members were obliged to defend their positions. Since the Convention did not take decisions by vote, the only way to secure a critical mass of support among its members was to reason and convince.

From beginning to end, the Convention never resorted to a vote. The Secretary General of the Convention played an essential role in this respect, keeping track of the interventions of the various members of the assembly to verify whether converging positions could be discerned. It was then for Giscard, Amato or Dehaene, either individually or in collaboration, to indicate the points on which a consensus had emerged (and how solid the consensus appeared) and the areas in which there remained divergent views. Obviously, this task required tact and sensitivity, and Giscard was often reproached for neglecting particular interventions. In the course of one plenary session, some speakers even indicated that they had counted more than forty dissenting interventions to show that the Convention was hostile to a certain proposal. With more than two hundred participants, such a number signified but a small minority (and in any case what counted was not votes but reasons). Nevertheless, those accustomed to parliamentary assemblies regarded the system as being undemocratic.

Apart from making it possible to avoid the trap of resorting to options, which would have limited the relevance of the Convention's work, the absence of a voting procedure had another essential advantage. According to the Laeken Declaration, "[t]he accession candidate countries will be fully involved in the Convention's proceedings. They will be [. . .] able to take part in the proceedings without, however, being able to prevent any consensus which may emerge among the Member States." If the Convention had taken decisions by vote, the representatives of the Member States-to-be would have been constantly exposed to discriminatory treatment. Not only would their votes have been counted separately, but indeed their votes would have been taken into account only if they were consistent with the majority of the other members.

Proceeding without any voting procedure yielded yet another advantage: it permitted a maximum exploitation of the Convention's rich composition. Under the circumstances, the contributions and proposed amendments of the alternates and of the observers were given as much weight as the official members. The alternates not only included many distinguished individuals with extensive experience, but some of them followed the proceedings more attentively than their official counterparts. In the midst of the Iraq crisis, for example, the French and German Foreign Ministers could not simultaneously be at the UN Security Council in New York and at the Convention in Brussels.

Finally, the avoidance of votes deprived those members seeking to derail the Convention of a redoubtable weapon. Indeed, if it had been necessary to vote on every amendment proposed, it would have been easy to multiply their number. One member in particular submitted hundreds of proposals to substitute the term "Community" for that of "Union". The assembly would have had to vote in machine-gun fashion as the European Parliament does, without any time to discuss the proposals' merits. The resulting image of the Convention in the mind of the public would have been disastrous.

With an assembly so generously populated, and in the absence of a voting procedure to structure the debate, draconian rules had to be enforced to give everyone a chance to express his or her own opinion. Without limits on the time permitted for interventions, the Convention could have been held hostage to the stalling tactic known across the Atlantic as "filibustering". This technique has been used by certain US Congressmen to prolong their intervention for as long as possible, using any trick they can think of – for example, reading from the Bible – to frustrate the continuation of the debate. It's easy to imagine the opponents of a proposal reciting passages from the Treaties or from the thousands of pages of reports produced in the last half-century to drive forward the construction of Europe.

Consequently, during the plenary sessions, intervening speakers were limited to a maximum of three minutes, provided they had reserved such time in advance through the Secretariat. If, during the course of a session, a member who had not reserved any time changed his mind and decided to address the floor, he or she had a blue card with which to attract the attention of the Presidency and of the Secretary General. Such extemporaneous interventions were limited to just one minute. A chronometer displayed the number of seconds elapsed in great big red numbers.

The main disadvantage to this approach was that it encouraged a succession of monologues instead of real debate, to the disappointment of those who appreciate lively verbal jousting. However, the president of the session was able to spice up the discussion in two ways. On the one hand, he could decide to yield the floor to a few impromptu, *blue card* speakers in between two reserved interventions. On the other hand, if necessary he could refuse to let an alternate speak if the relevant official member was present in the room.

Many spectators must have been disappointed, and journalists often didn't know what to report on after seeing the debates. This was because, as a result of the Convention's consensus-oriented method, the interventions functioned more as a sort of surrogate vote than as contributions to an authentic debate. Nevertheless, it should not be forgotten that the oral proceedings were supplemented by the abundant written contributions of the participants, which were immediately distributed by e-mail and posted on the website of the Convention. It was by way of this written input that a fundamental part of the debate was carried out.

5.2. The President's Chinese Turtle

The Laeken Declaration provided that the Convention was to hold its inaugural session on 1 March 2002 and to conclude "after a year, that is to say in time for the Chairman of the Convention to present its outcome to the European Council". At a maximum, the Convention thus had until the summit that was to mark the end of the Greek Presidency of the Council in June of 2003. After four months of work, many members, and most analysts, had the impression that the Convention was going nowhere and that it was getting bogged down in its own discussions. Then, in June of 2002, Giscard responded to the criticisms of members of the assembly by bringing into the room his Chinese ceramic turtle, a symbol of both slowness and tenacity, and by promising that the turtle would accompany the Convention to the end of the road.

Calendar of the Convention Proceedings

28 February 2002	Inaugural session	Inaugural discourse; discussion of internal rules
March – October 2002	Seventeen half-day plenary sessions	"Listening phase"; organisation of working groups
October 2002 – January 2003	Nine half-day plenary sessions	Presentations of the working groups and of the "skeleton" of the Constitution
February – April 2003	Twelve half-day plenary sessions	Presentation of the first preliminary draft Articles; first amendments; discussions in plenary
May – June 2003	Seven half-day plenary sessions	Amendments; discussions; adoption by consensus of Parts I and II (13 June 2003)

Calendar of the Convention Proceedings (Cont'd)

20 June 2003	European Council in Thessaloniki;	Presentation of the Constitution (Parts I and II)
June – July 2003	Two plenary sessions; concluding session	Adoption of Parts III and IV; Signature of the members of the Convention (all members signed except for four official members and four alternates)
18 July 2003	Official ceremony in Rome	Completed text delivered to the President of the European Council

As the Presidency had explained from the beginning, it was envisaged that the work would be pursued in three phases, namely:
- A *"listening phase*: identification of the expectations and needs of the Member States, their governments and parliaments, and those of European society";
- A *"deliberating phase*: comparison of the various opinions put forward and assessment of their implications and consequences"; and
- A *"proposing phase*: synthesis and drafting of proposals".

The "listening phase" concluded with the summer vacation in 2002. The "deliberating phase" and the "proposing phase" largely overlapped because, as early as 28 October 2002, the Praesidium presented the structure of the future Treaty – which Giscard was fond of calling a *squelette* ("skeleton") – to the members of the Convention.

Looking back, it can be seen that the subdivision of the Convention's work into three phases essentially served two functions. First of all, it helped to establish the legitimacy of the Convention: it clearly did not aim at producing yet another report by experts or *wise men* based on their own knowledge and experience but was instead designed to elicit the expectations of the citizens of the Union and to translate them into proposals. Such an approach was essential, because none of the members of the Convention had been directly elected as representatives of the people, which posed a problem since politicians no longer receive blank checks from their constituencies in a representative democracy and since the media are inept and ineffective at explaining Europe to the public. Only time will tell whether the efforts made by the Convention to address its democratic dilemma were successful.

According to the Laeken Delaration, "[t]he Chairman will pave the way for the opening of the Convention's proceedings by drawing conclusions from the public debate". It is easy to imagine the criticism that would have been levelled at Giscard – already accused as he was of authoritarianism – if he had held to the letter of the Declaration and presented, right at the start of the Convention, his personal "conclusions from the public debate".

The second function served by dividing the work into three phases was to instil a group dynamic: the members of the Convention had to get to know each other and had to learn how to work together before the group could make important choices. This was another inevitable consequence of the decision to eschew voting in favour of a consensus of the assembly.

The disadvantage of the three-step *listening/deliberating/proposing* approach was that it obviously reduced the amount of time that could be devoted to drafting the Constitution. Indeed, the Praesidium did not undertake that task until the Christmas of 2002, leaving only about six months for the work to be accomplished. Six months may seem like a lot of time when compared to the thirteen days of the Convention of Herrenchiemsee, which produced the text of the future German Basic Law in August of 1948. As for the Philadelphia Convention in 1787, the delegates began their work on 25 May and a first draft of the US Constitution was ready by early August. A month later the assembly entrusted the document to a "Committee of Style and Arrangement", led by Gouverneur Morris, and on 17 September the delegates signed the final text. However, unlike the European Convention of 2002-2003, these earlier Conventions had a much more limited number of participants and, more importantly, they worked continuously, without shuttling to and from their constituent institutions and without taking vacations.

The members of the Convention could not remain permanently in Brussels, in large part because their legitimacy depended on their close contact with the institutions from whence they came. The Convention worked at a tempo of about two plenary sessions per month, each of which lasted half a day. In all, there were somewhat less than 50 full days of deliberation.

5.3. Working Groups and Discussion Circles

Most of the important decisions of Convention, beginning with the decision to elaborate a draft Constitution Treaty to replace the Treaties of Rome and Maastricht, were taken on the basis of the preparations carried out by working groups. The creation of the working groups was decided by the Praesidium, generally in response to suggestions made from the floor during a plenary session or presented in the written contributions of the members of the Convention. The Praesidium specified the mandate of each working group and designated various *rapporteurs*, all of whom were members of the Praesidium itself, on the basis of their technical competence and experience in the field concerned.

Convention members participated in the working groups on a voluntary basis, with the Praesidium and the Secretariat ensuring that the composition of the groups reflected the various perspectives present in the Convention as a whole. The working groups held numerous hearings, in which both experts and university professors offered their input. The debates were less formal and much more thorough than those in the plenary sessions, and their impact on the Convention was unmistakable and crucial.

The role of the *rapporteur* was also essential, as it served to pose the right questions, to synthesise the discussions and to promote consensus within the working group. However, consensus was not always possible, as demonstrated by the limited progress made by the Convention in the field of economic governance.

Working Groups and Discussion Circles of the Convention

Working Group	Rapporteur	Issues examined
WG I: Subsidiarity	I. Méndez de Vigo	*Monitoring compliance with the principle of subsidiarity; possible monitoring mechanisms/procedures*
WG II: Charter of Fundamental Rights of the European Union (and the ECHR)	A. Vitorino	*Incorporation of the Charter of Fundamental Rights into the Treaty; implications of accession by the Community/Union to the European Convention on Human Rights*
WG III: Legal personality	G. Amato	*Explicit recognition of the EU's legal personality; merging the Union's legal personality with that of the Community; contribution of such innovations to the simplification of the Treaties*
WG IV: National parliaments	G. Stuart	*The role of national parliaments in the current architecture of the Union; the functioning of national arrangements; possible need to consider new mechanisms/procedures at national or Union level*
WG V: Complementary competences	H. Christophersen	*Future treatment of "complementary" competences; whether Member States should be accorded full competence for matters in which the Union presently has complementary competence, or whether the limits of the Union's complementary competence should be spelled out*
WG VI: Economic governance	K. Hänsch	*Possible forms of economic and financial cooperation to respond to the introduction of the Euro*
WG VII: External action	J.L. Dehaene	*Defining and formulating the interests of the Union; ensuring coherence of the Union's external action; coordination of all the instruments at the Union's disposal; possibility of extending the Community method to other fields of action; etc.*
WG VIII: Defence	M. Barnier	*Ensuring effective crisis management and responses to terrorism; ensuring that Member States meet their commitments as regards military capabilities; whether the Treaty should provide for collective defence, possibly with an opt-in clause*
WG IX: Simplification	G. Amato	*Reducing the number of and simplifying legislative procedures; reducing the number of legal instruments referred to in the Treaties; possibility*

Working Groups and Discussion Circles of the Convention (Cont'd)

Working Group	Rapporteur	Issues examined
		of giving such procedures more comprehensible names; simplification of the budgetary procedure
WG X: Freedom, security and justice	J. Bruton	*Improvements necessary for genuine, full and comprehensive implementation of an area of freedom, security and justice; clearer identification of criminal law issues that require action at Union level; increased judicial cooperation in criminal matters; adjustments to the Treaty provisions defining the Community's competence in regard to immigration and asylum matters*
WG XI: Social Europe	G. Katiforis	*Basic values in the social field; inclusion of social objectives; possible modifications of the present competences of the Union/Community in social matters; role of the "open method of coordination" and its possible inclusion in the Constitution; the link that could be established between economic policy and social policy coordination; possible extension of co-decision and qualified majority voting; the role of the social partners*
Discussion circle on the Court of Justice	A. Vitorino	*Consequences of enlargement on the composition and functioning of the ECJ; possible changes to the grounds for bring legal actions under the three pillars; possible changes to the procedure for appointing Judges and Advocates General; appointment of members of the CFI; possible changes to the names of the ECJ and the CFI; whether the wording of the fourth paragraph of Article 230 EC concerning direct appeals by individuals against general acts of the Institutions should be amended; whether and how to make the system of penalties for non-compliance with a judgment of the ECJ more effective*
Discussion circle on the budgetary procedure	H. Christophersen	*Improvement and simplification of the budgetary procedure and the consequences of the distinction between "compulsory" and "non-compulsory" expenditures; incorporation of the financial perspectives into the Constitution; procedure for adopting the multi-annual perspectives*
Discussion circle on own resources	I. Méndez de Vigo	*Whether the existing system of own resources meets public expectations in terms of fairness and transparency; whether Council decisions under the Article 269 procedure should continue to be unanimous; the role of the European Parliament; Whether the Article 269 procedure should maintain the requirement for adoption by the Member States according to their constitutional*

Working Groups and Discussion Circles of the Convention (Cont'd)

Working Group	Rapporteur	Issues examined
		requirements, or whether financing should be a Union competence; whether the existing decision-making procedure would allow substantial amendments to be made to these resources

Once the work on a draft text had begun, the Praesidium also created "discussion circles", each of which was charged with studying technical questions and proposing detailed solutions. Even more than for the working groups, the composition of the discussion circles was determined by the technical competence of the participants in the relevant fields. However, at least from the outside the difference between the two types of groups appears minimal, especially as regards their final products.

5.4. From Rough Sketch to the Convention's Final Text

The drafting of the various Articles of the Convention's text can be broken down into ten or so different phases. The Praesidium and the Secretariat played pivotal roles. All the work was done under intense time pressure. The members of the Convention had, on average, one week between the time they were apprised of the draft text and the deadline for presenting amendments if they wanted these to be taken into consideration for the following plenary session. To be admitted, such amendments had to have the form of a draft text, accompanied by a brief statement of reasons. Many of the members complained that, due to these relentless deadlines, they lacked the time necessary to consult their institution of origin. However, the quality of the numerous amendments, and of the justifications supporting them, reflect the substantial work that was done to the text and indicate that those governments and parliaments that were well organised managed to put the strict timetable to good use.

In the end, the brisk pace of the work was both advantageous in that it contributed to the coherence of the text as a whole and at the same time led to many minor drafting errors and inconsistencies.

Ten Phases of Drafting the Convention's Text

1. Preparation of a rough sketch by the Secretariat
2. Discussion by the Praesidium and drafting of a definitive first draft
3. Presentation of the text in plenary with the comments of the President and publication of the text on the Convention's website
4. Proposals for amendments presented by the members of the Convention
5. Synthesis of amendments by the Secretariat
6. Debate in plenary

---

7. Where necessary, re-drafting of the text in light of the debate in plenary to integrate the amendments, in accordance with phases 1 to 3.
8. Where necessary, a new debate and survey of consensus by the Presidency
9. Ordering and re-numbering of the draft
10. General debate and survey of consensus with respect to the entire text (10 June 2003 - 18 July 2003)

The contrast with the IGCs is striking. Indeed, the government representatives at the ICGs have at their full disposal the experts of the Legal Service of the Council, at the highest level, and may organise working meetings among the experts of the Council, the governments of the Member States and the Commission. The IGCs the work is furthermore carried out in only two or three languages until the meeting of the European Council. By contrast, the Convention's team of drafters were very enthusiastic but often young and less experienced, and the drafts were presented in plenary in all eleven of the EU's official languages. The IGC system is thus seemingly more efficient. However, the advantages of the IGC have been no guarantee against the many and occasionally significant divergences between the different linguistic versions of the Treaties and other inconsistencies that have become apparent with the passage of time.

Part II of the Constitution was of course ready for insertion from the very beginning. As explained earlier, this second part consisted simply of the text of the Charter of Fundamental Rights that had been "proclaimed" at Nice in December of 2000.

Part III was the result of a more complex process. The Praesidium engaged a group of six experts, chosen from the members of the Legal Services of the Council, the Commission and the European Parliament, to carry out the preparatory work. The Commission's experts had already been part of the team that drafted the *Penelope* document. The six experts responded to the two detailed mandates they were given with reports that were rather voluminous but extremely interesting, particularly for jurists. The experts combed over all the provisions of the Treaties of Rome and Maastricht to identify any changes logically necessary in light of the Convention's decisions with respect to Part I. The experts also presented a series of proposals for the reorganisation of the texts. For the most part these were followed to the letter, although the Praesidium added many more substantial modifications, most of which followed from the recommendations of the working groups and discussion circles. The final result was not only impressive from a quantitative point of view but was also much more innovative than the output of the preceding IGCs.

5.5. The Most Transparent Constitutional Process Ever

One of the distinguishing features of the Convention is that, upon approval by the Praesidium, the texts were immediately made available to anyone interested. By contrast, notes and relevant materials used by the Praesidium prior to adopting such texts were jealously guarded by the Secretary General to ensure that the Praesidium had complete freedom to deliberate internally. Despite these efforts to maintain secrecy, however, when the process grew more politicised, leaks began to emerge as certain members of the Praesidium started consulting their respective political parties. Convention members not linked to any such party were thus on various occasions unpleasantly surprised to read about a new proposed text in the press before finding a copy of it on their table at the Convention.

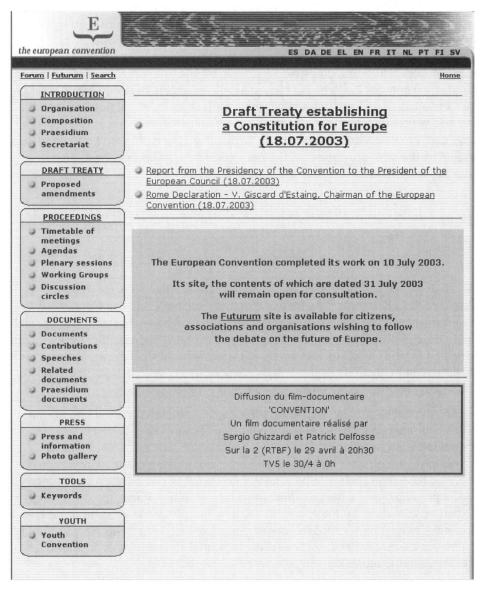

That said, it must be stressed that never before has there been any more transparent process for the elaboration of a draft Constitution. Those who, in the final weeks of the Convention railed against its elitist character had clearly paid little attention to all the documents that were already available on the Convention's website – which moreover was remarkably well organised in comparison to many others. In addition, many critics confused the character of the Secretariat's necessarily discreet preparatory work – which had no political legitimacy – with that of the work that followed in the Praesidium and in plenary. These critics were furthermore plainly inept in drawing appropriate comparisons: while it is true that, in other analogous settings, one could simultaneously access the official reports of the work carried out in committees and in plenary, this was not possible until long after the work had been completed.

One final note for lawyers and historians: the ensemble of documents posted on the Convention's website will remain there until at least July of 2008. These documents, which include nearly two thousand contributions, notes, reports, draft texts and proposals for amendments, will make it possible to reconstruct the origins of the new provisions and, where necessary, to retrace the Convention's thinking and "intent".

6. THE ICG: A FEW STEPS FORWARD, A FEW STEPS TO THE REAR

6.1. From Rome to Brussels

On 18 July 2003, Valéry Giscard d'Estaing passed the baton to Italian Prime Minister Silvio Berlusconi. As Italy at that time held the European Council's rotating Presidency, it was Berlusconi's responsibility to organise the Intergovernmental Conference, with a view toward debating and adopting the text that Giscard had presented to the Council in Thessaloniki. The revision of the Treaties of Rome and of Maastricht by the IGC is governed by Article 48 (ex-Article N) of the Treaty of Maastricht (i.e., the Treaty on European Union), which provides:

> The government of any Member State or the Commission may submit to the Council proposals for the amendment of the Treaties on which the Union is founded.
>
> If the Council, after consulting the European Parliament and, where appropriate, the Commission, delivers an opinion in favour of calling a conference of representatives of the governments of the Member States, the conference shall be convened by the President of the Council for the purpose of determining by common accord the amendments to be made to those Treaties. The European Central Bank shall also be consulted in the case of institutional changes in the monetary area.

The amendments shall enter into force after being ratified by all the Member States in accordance with their respective constitutional requirements.

Already at Nice in December of 2000, the European Council had decided to open another IGC, and this decision was reaffirmed the following year at Laeken. All that remained, following the Convention, was to set it into motion.

Observers awaited the IGC with both hope and trepidation, regardless of their judgement of the Convention's text. Some hoped that the Member States would push the text farther in the direction of a federalist or functionalist system but feared that they would take a decidedly more intergovernmentalist turn. Others hoped, to the contrary, that the Member States would limit the scope of the innovations introduced by the Convention and adopt new provisions favouring sectoral or other special interests. The Spanish and Polish governments had already indicated, in July of 2003, that they did not want to lose the voting advantage they had acquired by virtue of the Treaty of Nice, incompatible as it was with the *double majority*-based system of qualified majority voting proposed by the Convention.

The success of an IGC depends largely on the government of the Member State that occupies the Presidency of the Union, as it is the President that controls the agenda and hence the timetable. Moreover, it is the President that can decide – normally with the agreement of the other members of the European Council – whom to invite to attend the IGC's proceedings in the capacity of observers.

In 1991, the Luxembourgish and Dutch Presidencies demonstrated how important this leadership role is for the IGC. During the summer, the Dutch Minister of Foreign Affairs decided to put aside a draft text, prepared in the preceding semester by his counterpart from Luxembourg, around which a wide consensus had already formed. When the new Dutch text appeared, with its distinctively more federalist tenor, a crisis arose in the negotiations, which cost the IGC substantial time and which abated only when the Dutch Presidency decided to put the Luxembourgish text back on the agenda. However, instead of five months, only one month remained before the summit of Maastricht, where the Dutch government wanted the Treaty to be adopted. This explains some of the shaky solutions in the Maastricht Treaty, which was not signed until 7 February 1992.

The essential point regarding the IGC is that everything is in the hands of the national governments: whatever the clout of the Commission, which has for a long time been participating at the IGCs as an observer, or of the European Parliament, whose representatives were invited to the last two IGCs, these Institutions attend the IGC totally unarmed. By contrast, each of the governments has the right to stop a proposal in its tracks with a veto.

This was the danger that threatened the work of the Convention. Although the Convention's text had many imperfections, on the whole it was cohesive and delicately balanced. If one of its provisions were modified significantly, the entire structure could collapse like a house of cards, or at best the text could emerge disfigured and asymmetrical.

In any case, the IGC did not have the last word, given the need for ratification in each Member State, and this was both a handicap and an opportunity. It was a handicap in the sense that many governments feared the consequences of the ratification process and wanted to be able to return home and declare victory – even if a Pyrrhic one, as was seen at Nice. At the same time, this was an opportunity because, if necessary, the Convention's defenders could appeal to public opinion: how dare the IGC go behind closed doors and pick apart the work realised with maximum transparency by hundreds of legitimate representatives of the citizens and the institutions of the Member States?

Such an appeal was not necessary, despite concerns that arose when the IGC decided to reject the idea of a Legislative Council (which would have been a separate configuration of the Council of Ministers, meeting and deliberating in public when the Council acts in its capacity as legislator). The Convention's text enjoyed the strong support of Italy: not only the support of the government but also of the opposition, not to mention that of Giuliano Amato and of Commission President Romano Prodi. Indeed, all of the key Italian figures did their best to convey the idea that the Convention's text had to be adopted with only those amendments that were indispensable for technical or political reasons. This explains why, despite the failure of the Brussels summit in December of 2003 during the Italian Presidency, the Constitution emerged from the IGC relatively intact and was signed on 29 October 2004 – in the same room where, on 25 March 1957, the original six Member States had signed the Treaties of Rome.

The work of the IGC commenced officially on 4 October 2003, but there had already been an informal meeting of the Foreign Ministers in Riva del Garda in Italy on 5 and 6 September of that year. After a cooling off period following deadlock at the Brussels summit, the Member States were finally able to agree on a final text and conclude the IGC on 18 June 2004, the anniversary of the Battle of Waterloo, fought near Brussels in 1815 (and for that matter, the anniversary of De Gaulle's appeal from London to the French in 1940 to keep fighting alongside the British).

Meetings of the Intergovernmental Conference of 2003-2004

2003:	
5-6 September	*Riva del Garda, Italy: informal gathering of the Foreign Ministers*
4 October	Rome: official launch of the IGC
13 October	Luxembourg: meeting of the Foreign Ministers
16 October	Brussels: meeting of the heads of State and governments
27 October	Brussels: meeting of the Foreign Ministers
18 November	Brussels: meeting of the Foreign Ministers

28-29 November	Naples: *conclave* of the Foreign Ministers
8 December	Brussels: meeting of the Foreign Ministers
12-13 December	Brussels: European Council and summit of the heads of State and governments on the Constitution
2004:	
24 March	*Brussels: European Council and report of President Ahern on the prospects of reopening the IGC*
4 May	Dublin: "focal points" meeting of the Foreign Ministers
17-18 May	Brussels: meeting of the Foreign Ministers
24 May	Brussels: meeting of the Foreign Ministers
14 June	Luxembourg: meeting of the Foreign Ministers
17-18 June	Brussels: European Council and summit of the heads of State and governments on the Constitution

6.2. The Return of the Experts

Beginning in the summer of 2003, the Secretariat General of the Council had already carried out the technical work necessary to clean up the Convention's text, filling gaps and correcting mistakes, which the Secretariat of the Convention could not do for lack of time. It was this revised text, published on 25 November 2003 (document 50/03 CIG) although completed earlier, which served as the basis for the political discussions within the IGC. For the most part this text was essentially the same as the Convention's text. The only alterations were of no legal consequence but were designed to achieve more homogeneous formulations and hence a smoother style. However, the Council's experts did complete a certain number of Articles in Part III, in particular those relating to the choice of legal instruments (i.e., laws versus regulations) that had been left aside by the Convention, either as an oversight or by design.

The most spectacular change was the relocation of the provision relating to the principle of the primacy of Union law over that of the Member States. First of all, the essence of Article 10(2), which reaffirmed the duty of sincere cooperation on the part of the Member States, was moved to up to Article I-5(2) (*Relationship between the Union and the Member States*), which states, *inter alia*, that "[t]he Member States shall take any appropriate measure, general or particular, to ensure fulfilment of the obligations arising out of the Constitution or resulting from the acts of the institutions of the Union". As for the principle of primacy itself, the contents of Article 10(1) were moved up to Article I-6 (*Union law*), according to which "[t]he Constitution and law adopted by the institutions of the Union in exercising competences conferred on it shall have primacy over the law of the Member States". The principle of primacy thus appears in Title I, *Definitions and objectives of the Union*, instead of Title III, *Union Competences*, where it had been situated by the Convention.

To some readers, the relocation of the primacy clause might give the impression that, by virtue of Article I-6, the Constitution and the laws of the Union take precedence over the law of the Member States in a *general and absolute* sense, i.e., in a manner analogous to the national context where the constitution of a sovereign State prevails over that State's laws and regulations. By contrast, in the Convention's text, primacy appeared more like a principle applicable to the exercise of competences, comparable in this regard to the principles of conferral, subsidiarity and proportionality. In any event, whether or not the new location of the clause entails any legal consequences – which remains to be seen – it seems fair to predict that its new home in Title I will be controversial in certain national debates concerning ratification. Not much clearer, either for lawyers or for the public at large, is the meaning of a declaration annexed to the Constitution according to which "[t]he Conference notes that Article I-6 reflects existing case law of the Court of Justice of the European Communities and of the Court of First Instance". To apply this declaration in concrete circumstances, one not only needs to be familiar with the case law of the European Courts in this area, but also needs to divine the significance of the word "reflects".

A comparison between the final text of the Constitution and the text produced by the Convention will provoke different reactions from the reader depending on which linguistic version one uses. The French version of the Convention's text, which by 18 July 2003 had already been corrected stylistically and grammatically by the *Académie française*, is the one to which the fewest changes were made. The other linguistic versions had been drafted hurriedly during the Convention to enable its members to familiarise themselves with the issues on which they had to take a position. The IGC, on the other hand, carried out its work on the basis of the English and especially the French texts.

The text completed by the lawyers in the Secretariat General of the Council together with those of the Commission and of the 25 Member States is barely distinguishable from the text of the Convention. Most obviously, the numbering of the Articles changed. In addition, many formulations in the text were adjusted to render them more systematically repetitive – to sometimes lighter and sometimes heavier effect. Yet overall the texts are remarkably similar. One might imagine that the Convention's text would have been quite different in the first place if, instead of having its own Secretariat, the Convention had been assisted by the Secretariat of the Council, as contemplated by the Laeken Declaration. However, the Council's experts worked on the text, with a fresh mind, for an entire year (i.e., from September 2003 until September of 2004) and it essentially remained unchanged. This is a significant validation of the work done by the Secretariat and

Praesidium of the Convention, which moreover had only six months to work – under tremendous pressure – on a text in constant mutation.

6.3. *Diplomacy and "Conclaves"*

Article 48 of the Treaty of Maastricht does not specify who may represent the governments of the Member States at the IGC, nor does it indicate who may be invited to attend. In practice, the composition of particular meetings varies according to their purpose. With respect to the IGC that approved the Constitution, one representative from the Commission and one from the European Parliament were in attendance. However, they had no vote and no ability to veto any proposal, since the IGC is a conference between States. The IGC met thirteen times in two different configurations: nine times, after the informal gathering at Riva del Garda, at the level of Foreign Minister (i.e., five times under the Italian Presidency in 2003 and four times under the Irish Presidency in 2004) and four times at the level of heads of State and government (three times under the Italian Presidency and once under the Irish Presidency). Considering the reduced number of points in discussion, not to mention the preparatory work and accompaniment of the experts, a comparison with the Convention does not appear, in terms of efficiency, to be very favourable to the IGC.

There are two principal reasons explaining the slowness of the IGC. The first reason, with which the public is more familiar, relates to the issues that received attention in the press. On the one hand, there were the positions taken by the Spanish and Polish governments, who were hostile to the Convention's *double majority* formula for qualified majority voting. On the other hand, there was the resistance on the part of several governments – essentially those of the small and new Member States, whose cause was supported by Commission President Prodi – to any deviation from the principle of "one Commissioner for every Member State". The second reason, much less well known, is that the Ministers of Finance attempted to limit the budgetary powers of the European Parliament, while many of the Foreign Ministers made a series of specific demands to modify the text to protect sectoral and national interests. While resisting these attempts for the most part, the Italian Presidency, under the direction of Foreign Minister Franco Frattini, sought to keep to the road it had fixed. Frattini's desire was to secure the approval of the Convention's text essentially intact but with two improvements that were also advocated by the Commission: an extension of qualified majority voting to additional fields; and a simplified procedure for revising Part III of the Constitution.

The key meeting during the Italian Presidency was undoubtedly the so-called *conclave* of Naples of 28-29 November 2003. By the end of that meeting, the Foreign Ministers had been unable to find a compromise on the issues of qualified majority voting and the composition of the Commission. As for the other contentious points, the Presidency had managed to convince the group to accept a certain number of innovations, subject to a final agreement on the entire package. However, progress on these points came at the price of compromises which mostly enhanced the Member States' power to block future changes to the Union's policies and to the Constitution.

All things considered, when the European Council convened in Brussels on 12-13 December 2003, the path to a final accord seemed to have been cleared.

6.4. Summit Vertigo

Ever since 1985, when the Single European Act was adopted under the Council President then in rotation, namely Italian Prime Minister Giulio Andreotti, the most delicate questions concerning the revision of the Treaties have always been handled personally by the heads of State, often during long and gruelling meetings lasting until the wee hours. The negotiating abilities of the participants – or, in the absence thereof, their ability to surround themselves with consummate diplomats and to listen to them – has always played an important role in such meetings. However, the Nice summit of December 2001 demonstrated the limits and dangers of this kind of decision making.

The Italian Presidency in 2003 appeared to have a certain taste for summits, organising three of them in little more than three months under the close watch of television cameras and the press. It will never be known whether another President would have been able to find a compromise through negotiation, but in any event, rather than seeking a negotiated solution, Berlusconi chose to throw in the towel when faced with the apparently irreconcilable positions of the Spanish Prime Minister José María Aznar and French President Jacques Chirac – to cite only the most spectacular clash. Paradoxically, however, the failure to reach an accord on 13 December 2003 can be credited for underscoring the importance of one of the most distinctive innovations in the Constitution, namely the change from a six-month Presidency to a more stable Presidency with a (renewable) term of 2.5 years. Indeed, Berlusconi – realising that the baton would be passed to his Irish counterpart at the beginning of 2004, had less motivation to invest still more time and effort in thorny negotiations, particularly when he had already secured the European Council's agreement to situate the new European Food Safety Authority in Parma. A President with a more permanent mandate, presumably less preoccupied with placating voters in periodic national elections, will be able to devote his or her attention instead to the business of the European Council, in particular the medium-range shaping of the policies of the Union.

The failed summit of 12-13 December 2003 may have been advantageous in another respect as well. At the time, many politicians and specialists sympathetic to the federalist or functionalist visions of Europe complained that, due to the tradeoffs made during the IGC, the Constitution did not go far enough toward greater integration. The breakdown at the summit in fact set the stage, as it were, for another bite at the apple. In early 2004, the Irish Presidency showed patience, discretion and a spirit of compromise, meeting bilaterally with heads of State while, in Spain, political upheaval led to a new government and a somewhat different attitude toward negotiations in the IGC. In June, on the eve of the European Council in Brussels, the necessary compromises had ripened. Although the politicians and the media did not fail to deliver the required dose of drama and suspense at the last minute, few cognoscenti were surprised when the summit approved the text in relatively short order, and with minimal variations from what the Irish Presidency had proposed a few days earlier.

For those who had followed the protracted negotiations of the IGC and were impatiently awaiting a constitutional architecture that would enhance the functioning of the Union, the natural reaction, when the text was adopted on 18 June 2004, was: *it was about time!* And happily the essence of the Convention's text had been maintained. However, with some exceptions, the changes the IGC did make rendered the text more rigid – for the sole purpose of protecting national interests. A good illustration of this was the decision to increase the threshold percentages used in the definition of a qualified majority in the Council of Ministers. For example, instead of a requirement of 50% of the Member States representing 60% of the Union's population, which had been the Convention's proposed definition of a qualified majority for legislation in most policy areas, the thresholds were changed to 55% and 65% respectively.

Certain other aspects of the retreat of the IGC from the Convention's proposals are more difficult for non-experts to discern. For example, the *passerelle* ("bridging clause") permitting the Council to bypass unanimity requirements and to vote instead by qualified majority was made more rigid (see pages 36–37). Moreover, at the request of the UK, the *passerelle* may not be used for the harmonisation of social security and the social protection of workers (Article III-210(3)), although one has to be a skilled interpreter of procedural regulations to pick up on this. Three other steps backward are more serious from a structural point of view.

First, whereas the Convention had sought to clarify the legislative procedure, specifying that the European Council "shall not exercise legislative functions" – a provision that was maintained in Article I-21 – the IGC decided that the European Council should in fact have a role in the adoption of European laws regarding judicial cooperation in criminal matters (Articles III-270 and III-271). Second, the Convention had tried to remedy the instability caused by the revolving Presidency of the Council by providing that the Presidency of the various configurations of the Council should remain in place for at least a year. However, the IGC, after having rejected the Convention's proposal for a separate Legislative

Council, agreed on an extremely complex system for the Presidency (apart from the Presidency of the Foreign Affairs Council, to be chaired by the Foreign Minister of the Union) which, in effect, reaffirms the principle of a semi-annual rotation. Finally and most importantly, the IGC was unable to accept the Convention's proposal, as written, of a streamlined Commission of reduced size, perhaps due to the surprising support of the Prodi Commission for the principle of one Commissioner for every Member State. The Convention's proposal, which envisaged a group of non-voting Commissioners in addition to fifteen voting Commissioners, was already an unsatisfying compromise. The solution adopted by the IGC, which retains the "one Commissioner per Member State" principle, is worse still. Fortunately, this formula will lapse in 2014, when the number of Commissioners will be capped at two-thirds the number of Member States.

However, the misguided modifications made by the IGC, most of which stemmed from the Naples *conclave* of 28-29 November 2003 while others were conceived under the Irish Presidency, are trees that should not obscure the more promising forest. If one accepts the premise underlying this book, i.e, that the Constitution should be compared to the previous state of the art rather than to some ideal text, then it has to be concluded that overall – apart from the provisions regarding the composition of the Commission – the final text adopted on 18 June 2004 is a success no one could have imagined just two years before. Indeed, the IGC even managed to take the text farther than the Convention had in some respects. For example, a new "horizontal clause" was inserted which requires the Union "to take into account requirements linked to the promotion of a high level of employment, the guarantee of adequate social protection, the fight against social exclusion, and a high level of education, training and protection of human health" when defining and implementing the policies and actions referred to in Part III of the text (Article III-117). Another example, explained earlier at page 39, is the IGC's improvement of the procedure used when provisions contained in Part III are amended.

Most importantly, however, very many of the Convention's proposed solutions were never called into question: the simplification and democratisation of the legislative procedure; the demolition of the three-pillar system; and the majority of innovations contained in Part I, whether they concern the institutions of the Union or the participation of national parliaments. Furthermore, notwithstanding the PR-conscious spin of British Foreign Secretary Jack Straw, even the legally binding value of the Charter of Fundamental Rights was preserved. The IGC maintained, and in some cases enhanced, the protection of basic rights. On the other hand, it also reinforced the role of the Member States in a way that alters the institutional balance to the detriment of the functioning of the Union.

It has to be acknowledged that the IGC operated with unprecedented transparency. Indeed, the Italian Presidency decided to make public the proposals for amendments it put on the table by posting them on the internet, including both those it prepared itself and those submitted by this or that Member State. In May, when the IGC's work began again in earnest, the Irish Presidency maintained this practice. The public was thus able to follow the IGC as it progressed, although unfortunately only the specialists took full advantage of this opportunity. By contrast, the press concentrated its attention yet again on the more sensational aspects and on the divergent positions of the Member States, rather than on the substance and points of common ground. Furthermore, since it was an intergovernmental procedure, this also led the Member States to dig their foxholes too soon, as had already happened in connection with the Westendorp group as the Treaty of Amsterdam was being prepared. Transparency is not an absolute virtue: what worked for the Convention did not always prove suitable for the IGC. To be effective, diplomacy has to have a certain degree of discretion. Setting aside the issue of personal capacities, this was demonstrated by the comparison between the action of the Italian President of the European Council and the Irish President. The comparison also highlighted the flaws of the procedure for amending the Constitution, which maintains the requirement that an IGC be convened.

CHAPTER IV

WHAT EVERYBODY THINKS THEY KNOW . . .

1. . . . BUT WHAT ONLY THE FUTURE CAN SAY

A well-worn anecdote has it that Christopher Columbus dented the base of an egg to demonstrate that it could stand upright, apparently in defiance of the laws of physics. What few realise, however, is that the writings of Giorgio Vasari identify the author of this gesture as the Florentine architect Filippo Brunelleschi, who was born in 1377 (i.e., 74 years before Columbus) and had died prior to Columbus' return to Europe, when the latter reputedly got the egg to stand. According to Vasari, it was Brunelleschi who performed this egg magic while explaining how he proposed to cover the *Duomo* in Florence with an oval cupola.

Giscard d'Estaing and his companions can by no means be compared to Christopher Columbus – they certainly did not discover a new world. However, they do have much in common with Brunelleschi, in the sense that they sought to construct a harmonious and solid edifice. The cupola of *Santa Maria del Fiore* could only be placed atop the *Duomo* once the rest of the structure had been built, and the same may be said for the reforms made by the Convention to the Institutions, which were and will probably continue to be the focal point for the European press. Precisely because the institutional questions were the most volatile, the Praesidium avoided discussing them until the final weeks, when the rest of the Convention's essential work had been done and seemed sufficiently robust, and when the majority of the delegates seemed ready and willing to adopt a text.

However, the comparison with the *Duomo* of Florence ends here: the Institutions have neither its beauty, nor its coherence or harmony. In any event, several comments need to be made concerning the unique architecture of the Union and its recently renovated features.

The most spectacular changes concerning the Institutions inspired abundant commentary well before being adopted, and in the second half of the spring of 2003 these institutional innovations were the source of unprecedented tension in the Convention and in the Praesidium. Giscard, Amato and Dehaene knew very well they had reached the most difficult stretch of road, the same one where the national governments had already locked up their brakes on the way to Amsterdam and Nice. In early June, the tension was such that one of the plenary sessions had to be cancelled to allow political forces to get the ball rolling again. Giscard, who until that time had so often been accused of marching to the tune of the intergovernmentalists, was able to form an alliance with the parliamentarians to get the representatives of the national governments to face up to their responsibilities.

This tension was both the cause and the effect of the suspicions and the mental reservations that prevented a calm, rational evaluation of the innovations developed by the Convention. The significance of these innovations – taking into account the modifications introduced by the IGC – is very difficult to assess. Their true implications will only be revealed through practice and, for that matter, the compromise they reflect came at the price of several transitional measures. Many of the novel institutional provisions thus will not take effect until well into the second decade of this century.

1.1. A Seat for the President of the European Council

At present, the Presidency of the European Council rotates among the Member States every six months in an order fixed by the unanimous decision of the Council. The leadership responsibilities of the Presidency are assumed by the head of State or of the government of the Member State concerned. Many commentators maintained that the creation of a permanent Presidency of the European Council would destabilise the Community method in favour of the largest Member States. In support of this claim it was pointed out that the proposal for a permanent Presidency had been advanced, in various forms, by the British, Spanish and Italian Prime Ministers, by the German Chancellor and by the President of France. However, the possibility that this institutional change will bias the system is far from certain. On the one hand, the European Council will have to elect its President by a qualified majority ((Article I-22(1)), meaning that the large Member States will not likely be in a position to dictate who the President will be. On the other hand, once in office the President will be prohibited from holding any national office (Article I-22(3)) and hence will act independently of his or her national government.

European Constitution

Article I-22: The European Council President

1. The European Council shall elect its President, by a qualified majority, for a term of two and a half years, renewable once. In the event of an impediment or serious misconduct, the European Council can end his or her term of office in accordance with the same procedure.

2. The President of the European Council:
    (a) shall chair it and drive forward its work;
    (b) shall ensure the preparation and continuity of the work of the European Council in cooperation with the President of the Commission, and on the basis of the work of the General Affairs Council;
    (c) shall endeavour to facilitate cohesion and consensus within the European Council;
    (d) shall present a report to the European Parliament after each of the meetings of the European Council.

The President of the European Council shall, at his or her level and in that capacity, ensure the external representation of the Union on issues concerning its common foreign and security policy, without prejudice to the powers of the Union Minister for Foreign Affairs.

3. The President of the European Council shall not hold a national office.

In 1873, the French *Assemblée nationale* elected Patrice MacMahon as President of the Third Republic, and two years later gave him considerable powers, tailor-made for the expected return of the Bourbon dynasty. However, due to the political environment and to the strategic miscalculations of MacMahon, by 1877 the Presidents of the Third Republic had to content themselves with "inaugurating the chrysanthemums".

One implication of creating a permanent President is easy to foresee: the head of State or government serving as the European Council President will no longer have the simultaneous function of directing the policies of his or her own country while representing the Union *vis-à-vis* the leaders of third countries such as the United States. Other possible consequences of the new post will depend on the surrounding circumstances and the personalities occupying it.

1.2. A Union Minister for Foreign Affairs

Who remembers Vincent Auriol and Georges Bidault? In May of 1950, Auriol was the President of France and Bidault was the Prime Minister. But the French Foreign Minister at that time is well remembered indeed. His famous Declaration of 9 May 1950 is celebrated in Europe each year, and of course his name was Robert Schuman. On the other hand, who remembers the Foreign Ministers serving under Adenauer and de Gaulle when they signed the Franco-German Friendship Treaty in June of 1963?

Article I-28 of the Constitution establishes a Union Minister for Foreign Affairs. This is a new title for a relatively old function created in 1986 by Title III of the Single European Act, called at first "cooperation in the sphere of foreign policy" before being re-baptised as the "common foreign and security policy" (CFSP) in the Treaty of Maastricht in 1992. Article 30(5) of the Single European Act provided that "the external policies of the European Community and the policies agreed in European Political Co-operation must be consistent. The Presidency [i.e., the Member State holding the Presidency in rotation] and the Commission, each within its own sphere of competence, shall have special responsibility for ensuring that such consistency is sought and maintained." However, it took another decade before a dedicated post – namely, that of *Secretary-General of the Council, High Representative for the common foreign and security policy* – was established for the formulation and implementation of the CFSP by virtue of the Treaty of Amsterdam (Article 26 TEU). The continuity between the post of High Representative and the newly created Union Minister for Foreign Affairs is readily apparent, and indeed on 19 June 2004, when the European Council appointed the future President of the Commission (José Manuel Durao Barroso), it also confirmed that the current High Representative, Javier Solana Madariaga, would be nominated to fill the new post as soon as the Constitution enters into force.

The new Foreign Minister will clearly have an essential role. Ideally, he or she will be able to coordinate the CFSP while at the same time managing the Union's external action in the fields of commercial relations, aid to developing countries, and so on. Furthermore, the Foreign Minister will have to find ways to coordinate the external policies of the Union with those of the Member States. In this regard, the creation of a European External Action Service seems to be a clear signal of momentum towards better coordination. Originally proposed by the Convention as a Declaration to be annexed to the Constitution, the IGC actually went farther and transported the substance of the Declaration to Article III-296(3) of the final text.

European Constitution

Article III-296

3. In fulfilling his or her mandate, the Union Minister for Foreign Affairs shall be assisted by a European External Action Service. This service shall work in cooperation with the diplomatic services of the Member States and shall comprise officials from relevant departments of the General Secretariat of the Council and of the Commission as well as staff seconded from national diplomatic services of the Member States. The organisation and functioning of the European External Action Service shall be established by a European decision of the Council. The Council shall act on a proposal from the Union Minister for Foreign Affairs after consulting the European Parliament and after obtaining the consent of the Commission.

A tripartite External Action Service – involving the Council, the Commission and the Member States – will perhaps succeed where previous efforts in 1986, 1992, 1997 and 2001 failed, that is to say, it may be able to substitute real cooperation for competition between national diplomatic services, on the one hand, and between national services and those of the Commission, on the other. However, reality being what it is, there is no magic wand that can prevent occasional foreign policy disputes from arising between, for example, France and the UK, or between Portugal and Finland, or Belgium and Hungary, etc.

Part III of the Constitution also contains a reformulation of the CFSP (as complex as it is interesting) as well as the first traces of a common defence policy, which were reinforced by the IGC. Steps toward a common defence necessarily had to be cautious given that, at least in 2003, many governments were not ready to enter into military commitments at the European level, nor were the voters that had elected them. The sensitive nature of such a project is clear: for example, many Irish citizens voted no in the referendum of 2001 on the Treaty of Nice in the mistaken belief that the Treaty would compromise the policy of neutrality Ireland has observed since winning independence from the UK in January of 1922.

1.3. Weight-Loss Cure for a Bloated Commission

In 1972, the European Commission consisted of nine members. In 1985, when the programme to complete the internal market was launched, the membership had grown to fourteen. Until that time, simple group dynamics had permitted a collegial decision-making procedure that was indispensable for a cohesive vision of the general Community interest. Following the induction into the Community of Portugal and Spain in 1986 and of Austria, Finland and Sweden in 1995, the number of Commissioners stood at twenty. By virtue of a Protocol on the enlargement of the European Union, which was adopted together with the Treaty of Nice after long and difficult negotiations and which entered into force on 1 May 2004 on the basis of the Act of Accession of the ten new Member States, the Commission "shall include one national of each of the Member States". The Protocol further provides that, following the date of accession of the twenty-seventh Member State of the Union (i.e., most likely either Bulgaria or Romania in 2007 or 2008), "[t]he number of Members of the Commission shall be less than the number of Member States" and these Commissioners are to be "chosen according to a rotation system based on the principle of equality".

In the end, the divisive issue of the Commission's composition was not resolved until the very day the Constitution was adopted, i.e., 18 June 2004. Article I-26 of the Constitution, which lays down the relevant rules, may be summarised as follows:

- As from 1 May 2004, the Commission is to be composed of one Commissioner per Member State and the Commission that took up its duties in November of 2004 will remain in place without any changes if, as envisaged, the Constitution enters into force during its mandate (i.e., prior to November of 2009). The same rule will apply to the first Commission nominated following the Constitution's entry into force. With each future enlargement of the Union, there will be a new Commissioner for every new Member State. Therefore, if Bulgaria and Romania are joined by Croatia as the future medium-term additions to the Union, the Commission will likely have 28 members by October 2014 (if not more).
- Beginning on 1 November 2014, the number of Commissioners is to be equal to two thirds of the number of Member States, i.e., it is very likely to be 19 or 20, or about the size of the Commission under Romano Prodi, which consisted of 20 members. The number of Commissioners may be adjusted by the unanimous vote of the European Council. A rather complicated mechanism is established to ensure that each Member State is treated in the same manner with respect to the choice of Commissioners.

European Constitution:

Article I-26 (The European Commission)

1. [. . .]

2. [. . .]

3. The Commission's term of office shall be five years.

4. The members of the Commission shall be chosen on the ground of their general competence and European commitment from persons whose independence is beyond doubt.

5. The first Commission appointed under the provisions of the Constitution shall consist of one national of each Member State, including its President and the Union Minister for Foreign Affairs who shall be one of its Vice-Presidents.

6. As from the end of the term of office of the Commission referred to in paragraph 5, the Commission shall consist of a number of members, including its President and the Union Minister for Foreign Affairs, corresponding to two thirds of the number of Member States, unless the European Council, acting unanimously, decides to alter this number. The members of the Commission shall be selected from among the nationals of the Member States on the basis of a system of equal rotation between the Member States. This system shall be established by a European decision adopted unanimously by the European Council and on the basis of the following principles:

(a) Member States shall be treated on a strictly equal footing as regards determination of the sequence of, and the time spent by, their nationals as members of the Commission; consequently, the difference between the total number of terms of office held by nationals of any given pair of Member States may never be more than one;

(b) subject to point (a), each successive Commission shall be so composed as to reflect satisfactorily the demographic and geographical range of all the Member States.

[. . .]

The system adopted by the IGC was thus, in the end, a bit simpler than the compromise reached by the Convention, particularly because it does not create two classes of Commissioners, one with voting rights and one without. However, the IGC's solution is worse than that of the Convention, for at least two reasons.

Firstly, it defers action to address the problem until the long-term. Indeed, in the best scenario, this will lead to a series of crises with respect to the functioning of the Commission and, very possibly, to further tinkering with the Constitution. At worst, the new system will result, as in the past, in further complexity in the internal structures of the Commission's administration and increased tendencies to intervene in fields that are not priorities for the Union. Furthermore, it is conceivable that the Commission will find allies among Member States concerned about losing "their Commissioner" in order to ensure that the European Council prolongs the system as much as possible.

Secondly, by preserving, for several years, the principle of "one Commissioner for every Member State", the IGC has helped to reinforce the idea that the Commission, like the Council or the European Parliament, is an organ that represents the interests of individual Member States. This is a step backwards with respect to the conception of the European Community, for which the Commission was supposed to represent the general European interest according to a vision that was initially technocratic but which has become increasingly linked to the democratic process thanks to the growing influence of the Parliament. Indeed, the reality is that the Community and the Union suffer not so much from a "democratic deficit" as from a *management* deficit, which the system chosen by IGC does little to address.

The Prodi Commission, installed in the autumn of 1999, had already for some time shown a lack of internal cohesion which, as noted earlier, was evident even as regards the work of the Convention. Yet ironically, it was Romano Prodi himself who, together with the representatives of several of the new and "small" Member States, insisted stridently that there should continue to be one Commissioner per Member State. From the point of view of the President's ability to manage his team of Commissioners, this position defies explanation.

The solution adopted by the Convention was neither elegant nor easy to fathom. Article 25 of the text was an attempted compromise between the need for collegial action and the fear of many governments that, without their "own" Commissioner, their interests would not be properly understood by the Commission when taking decisions. According to Article 25, the number of "European Commissioners" was fixed at fifteen, including the Commission President and the Union's Foreign Minister. However, this core group of fifteen was joined by a group of "Commissioners", nominated by the President of the Commission, who were to have no voting rights. A complex rotation system for the "European Commissioners" was also provided for, as was a transitional regime that was to preserve the current composition of the Commission until 2009.

The question of whether the Commission should be chosen by the European Parliament or by the national governments was the subject of much bitter debate, both within the Convention and in the press and the specialised literature. Presently, the European Parliament elects the Commission President, and then, upon the President's proposal, the entire college of Commissioners. However, it is the European Council that has the crucial power to propose the candidate Commissioners in the first place.

If one compares Article I-27 of the Constitution with Articles 214 to 219 of the Treaty of Rome as modified by the Treaty of Nice – which took effect on 1 February 2003 and which thus applies to the Barroso Commission – it can be seen that, despite changes in the wording, the procedure for electing the Commission remains nearly the same. The accent is merely placed more squarely on the powers of its President.

Nomination of the Commission President before and after the European Constitution

Article I-27 of the Constitution: The President of the European Commission	Articles 214 and 217 of the Treaty of Rome (as amended by the Treaty of Nice)
Article 1-27	Article 214: [. . .]
1. Taking into account the elections to the European Parliament and after having held the appropriate consultations, the European Council, acting by a qualified majority, shall propose to the European Parliament a candidate for President of the Commission. This candidate shall be elected by the European Parliament by a majority of its component members. If he or she does not obtain the required majority, the European Council, acting by a qualified majority, shall within one month propose a new candidate who shall be elected by the European Parliament following the same procedure.	2. The Council, meeting in the composition of Heads of State or Government and acting by a qualified majority, shall nominate the person it intends to appoint as President of the Commission; the nomination shall be approved by the European Parliament.
2. The Council, by common accord with the President-elect, shall adopt the list of the other persons whom it proposes for appointment as members of the Commission. They shall be selected, on the basis of the suggestions made by Member States, in accordance with the criteria set out in Article I-26(4) and (6), second subparagraph.	The Council, acting by a qualified majority and by common accord with the nominee for President, shall adopt the list of the other persons whom it intends to appoint as Members of the Commission, drawn up in accordance with the proposals made by each Member State.
The President, the Union Minister for Foreign Affairs and the other members of the Commission shall be subject as a body to a vote of consent by the European Parliament. On the basis of this consent the Commission shall be appointed by the European Council, acting by a qualified majority.	The President and the other Members of the Commission thus nominated shall be subject as a body to a vote of approval by the European Parliament. After approval by the European Parliament, the President and the other Members of the Commission shall be appointed by the Council, acting by a qualified majority.
3. The President of the Commission shall:	*Article 217:*
(a) lay down guidelines within which the Commission is to work;	1. The Commission shall work under the political guidance of its President, who shall decide on its internal organisation in order to ensure that it acts consistently, efficiently and on the basis of collegiality.
(b) decide on the internal organisation of the Commission, ensuring that it acts consistently, efficiently and as a collegiate body;	2. The responsibilities incumbent upon the Commission shall be structured and allocated among its Members by its President. The President may reshuffle the allocation of those responsibilities during the Commission's term of office. The Members of the Commission shall carry out the duties devolved upon them by the President under his authority.

Article I-27 of the Constitution: The President of the European Commission	Articles 214 and 217 of the Treaty of Rome (as amended by the Treaty of Nice)
(c) appoint Vice-Presidents, other than the Union Minister for Foreign Affairs, from among the members of the Commission.	3. After obtaining the approval of the College, the President shall appoint Vice-Presidents from among its Members.
A member of the Commission shall resign if the President so requests. The Union Minister for Foreign Affairs shall resign, in accordance with the procedure set out in Article I-28(1), if the President so requests.	4. A Member of the Commission shall resign if the President so requests, after obtaining the approval of the College.

An examination of the functioning of the various parliamentary regimes in Europe and of the reforms to the procedure for nominating the President of the Commission yields one simple conclusion. The Constitution does not transform the Commission into a kind of government representing the majority of the Parliament, yet neither does it promote the vision of the Commission as an independent and relatively un-politicised organ serving to protect the general interests of the Union. The future relationship between the Commission and the Parliament will depend largely on the sense of legitimacy the parliamentarians have due to their election by popular vote. However, in the final analysis it will be, above all, the will of the majority of the national governments in the European Council that will continue to hold the keys to the election of the Commission. This is further illustrated by the decision of the European Council of 29 June 2004 (i.e., eleven days after it approved the Constitution) to anoint Barroso as President of the Commission that took office in November of that year. Furthermore, Article III-340 of the Constitution maintains the requirement of a two-thirds majority before Parliament can adopt a vote of no confidence *vis-à-vis* the Commission, which signifies that the Commission is not simply representative of the party or coalition that controls a majority in the European elections.

The Constitution does not specify whether the President of the European Council will be nominated prior to the nomination of the President of the Commission. However, the question is pertinent because both individuals will sit on the European Council and the first one nominated will therefore be in a position to influence the choice of the second. Resolution of this issue will depend in part on when the Constitution enters into force. If it enters into force on 1 November 2006, as envisaged by the text itself, the Commission President (and the Union's Foreign Minister) will in principle already have been nominated. On the other hand, if the ratification process resulted in a delay, both Presidents could possibly be named at the same time. An intense game of bargaining can very likely be expected between national governments and the political groups of the European Parliament to achieve a balanced solution from the standpoint of geographic and political factors. However, as pointed out previously, there are no legal obstacles that would prevent the same person from being nominated to fill the two posts simultaneously.

In any event, what will shape the future dynamics of the two Presidencies – perhaps to a greater extent than the actual terms of Article I-27 – will be the personalities of the relevant individuals, their personal and political ties with the national governments, and their ability to manage relationships with the European Parliament and with public opinion.

1.4. The Egg Spain Wouldn't Swallow: Double Majority Voting in the Council

Late into the night of 9 December 2000 at the summit of Nice, the heads of State and government discussed – rather un-diplomatically – the issue of how many votes each Member State would have, following enlargement, when meeting in the Council of Ministers. In the weeks preceding the summit, while France held the Presidency of the European Council, Jacques Chirac had refused to accept any scheme whereby France would have fewer votes in the Council of Ministers than Germany, despite the fact that reunification of the country had resulted in Germany having a population of about 80 million to France's 60 million. With great difficulty, the leaders finally agreed as to the relative voting weight each country would have. However, on the day following the long night of discussions it became evident that, in the heat of the moment, a computational error had been made. The result of the bargaining, once the error had been corrected, appeared in a "Protocol on the enlargement of the European Union", in a "Declaration on the enlargement of the European Union", and in a "Declaration on the qualified majority threshold and the number of votes for a blocking minority in an enlarged Union". The voting system described in these documents is of a complexity without precedent in the annals of European integration.

The best explanation of the origins and rationale of the weighted voting system used in the Council of Ministers is found in the *Memoirs* of Jean Monnet (chapter 14, section 2), where he refers to the drafting of the ECSC Treaty:

> The right to say no was the large countries' guarantee in their dealings with each other, and the smaller countries' safeguard against the large. The signature of the [ECSC Treaty] would be their last chance fully to exercise that negative right. Afterwards, they would enter an unknown world where the veto would be the exception and the rule of the majority would be law. But what majority? Four of the six countries – Italy and the three Benelux

countries – accounted for only a quarter of the Community's coal and steel production. It would not have been reasonable for them to be able to hold back France and Germany – which was what would happen if every country enjoyed one vote. That is why we proposed a system of weighted voting, to ensure that no decision could be imposed either by the combined power of France and Germany or by that of the other four.

Fifty years later, in spite of – or more probably because of – the experience gained since 1 July 1987, when the Single European Act entered into force and finally made it possible for the Council of Ministers to adopt decisions in many fields by a qualified majority, the basic utility of weighted voting remains the same, but the context has become somewhat more complex. First of all, the number of Member States has of course ballooned from six to twenty-five. Furthermore, the matters over which the Council of Ministers is competent to legislate are no longer limited to the production of coal and steel but cover the entire spectrum of the economy and touch on social policy, human rights, security and even foreign policy.

The solution adopted at Nice is a bad one, firstly because it is difficult to comprehend but also due to the jealousies and claims of unfairness it will continue to provoke whenever the number of votes assigned to the various Member States is compared to their respective populations. On the other hand, dissatisfaction on the part of some States is perhaps inevitable whenever a system of weighted voting is adopted.

A simple alternative to weighted voting, and an idea that has circulated for quite some time is voting by double majority. According to the double majority alternative, in order for the Council of Ministers (or the European Council, where it votes by a qualified majority) to adopt a measure, not only must a majority of the Member States be in favour of it, but those voting in favour must represent a majority of the population of the Union. If such a threshold is regarded as too low, the stipulated majority can simply be reinforced (e.g., by means of a two-thirds or three-fourths voting requirement) to prevent the Council from being held hostage by minority coalitions among the "Smalls" or the "Bigs".

The double majority solution, as expressed in Articles 24(1) and 24(2) of the Convention's text, not only made good sense but was also the logical consequence of the dual legitimacy of the Union, that is to say, the Union's links to the will of the Member States on the one hand and to the will of the people on the other. In the United States, the same twofold legitimacy is expressed both by the coexistence of the Senate and the House of Representatives and by the complex procedure by which the President is elected. In Europe, double majority voting is set within a broader institutional framework which itself reflects the Union's dual legitimacy, with the interests of the Member States represented by the European Council and the Council of Ministers while the people are represented by the European Parliament.

European Constitution

Article I-25: Definition of Qualified Majority within the European Council and the Council of Ministers

1. A qualified majority shall be defined as at least 55% of the members of the Council, comprising at least fifteen of them and representing Member States comprising at least 65% of the population of the Union.

A blocking minority must include at least four Council members, failing which the qualified majority shall be deemed attained.

2. By way of derogation from paragraph 1, when the Council does not act on a proposal from the Commission or from the Union Minister for Foreign Affairs, the qualified majority shall be defined as at least 72% of the members of the Council, representing Member States comprising at least 65% of the population of the Union.

3. Paragraphs 1 and 2 shall apply to the European Council when it is acting by a qualified majority.

4. Within the European Council, its President and the President of the Commission shall not take part in the vote.

In today's Union, composed of 25 Member States with 454 million inhabitants (as of 2004), a 65% majority of the population would correspond to about 295 million people. In principle, therefore, to muster a blocking minority it would be sufficient if the Member States opposing a measure represented a total population of 158.5 million people. The remaining issues to be decided are exactly which statistics to use and how frequently the relevant calculations are to be renewed.

According to the Convention's proposal, a qualified majority was defined as a simple majority of Member States representing three-fifths of the population of the Union (i.e., 272.5 million in 2004). However, this proposal could hardly have been received less enthusiastically by Spain and Poland, as it would have cancelled out the voting advantage they had acquired at Nice, whereby the number of votes assigned to them was clearly more than proportionate to their populations when compared to the votes of the largest Member States.

Votes of the Six Largest Member States (Final Act of the Nice Treaty)

Member State	Number of votes	Population
Poland	27	38.2 million
Spain	27	41.5 million
Italy	29	57.3 million
United Kingdom	29	59.3 million
France	29	59.6 million
Germany	29	82.5 million

Source: Eurostat yearbook 2004: the statistical guide to Europe. For the population of all of the Member States, see the table at pages 152–153.

The positions of Poland and Spain may have been dictated in part by complex calculations and scenarios – which seldom materialise – in which every vote cast in the Council of Ministers counts. On the other hand, it is equally possible that the chief concern of these countries was losing face before their electorates.

Against the obstinacy of Alfonso Dastis, the representative of the Spanish government and a member of the Praesidium, Giscard had only one weapon at his disposal: no double majority, no Constitution. Pressure from the other Convention members, particularly the parliamentarians, did the rest. However, the blows exchanged over this issue left their mark on the Convention's text in the form of a transitory regime that would have maintained the Nice Treaty's baroque voting system until 31 October 2009.

Those who believed that this compromise had definitively resolved the matter were in for a surprise. In July of 2003, the highest Spanish representatives announced that they would seek to re-open the question at the IGC. Polish Prime Minister Leszek Miller immediately followed suit. President Chirac and Chancellor Schröder, for their part, responded that they would not allow the work of the Convention to be undone. A new rupture between "old Europe" and "new Europe" thus emerged, but with one important difference: Prime Minister Blair was wary of becoming openly involved, and declared that he was very satisfied with the Convention's text. And Blair's manoeuvring was indeed in the best interests of the UK, considering that it obtained more concessions than any other Member State – both in the Convention and during the IGC.

As noted earlier, the rigidity of Spain and Poland on the one hand (which was compounded by the opposition of many of the smaller Member States to a slimmed-down Commission) and of France and Germany on the other led Council President Berlusconi, at the Brussels summit on 13 December 2003, to throw in the towel without trying to negotiate a settlement acceptable to all sides. However, by the time of the Brussels summit of 17-18 June 2004, the climate had changed. The dramatic March elections in Spain had shifted that country back toward the "old Europe" camp, and President Chirac could afford to soften his attitude somewhat because both the French regional elections in March and the European elections in early June had already been played out. The successful compromise proposed by Irish Prime Minister Ahern in Brussels on 18 June preserves the double majority system and thus guarantees the principle of equality among Member States and among citizens. At the same time, it excludes (at least on paper) the likelihood of a dominant voting bloc consisting of France, Germany and the UK: whereas the combined population of those three countries (i.e., about 200 million) would exceed 35% of the total population of the Union, Article I-25(1) of the Constitution specifies that proposals subject to qualified majority voting can only be defeated if they are opposed by a minimum of four Member States. The thresholds applying to the agreed double majority system are undoubtedly too high to guarantee rapid decision making. Nevertheless, the strengthening of the powers of the European Parliament, which will take a position on draft legislation before the Council of Ministers does, should have an important impact on the Member States' ability to find common ground.

2. . . . WHAT MAY BE SURMISED. . .

Two other innovations devised by the Convention, although less spectacular than the double majority voting regime, have attracted abundant commentary. As with other features new to the Union, the consequences of these innovations will depend on how they are practically applied. However, in this case it is easier to hazard some predictions based on the current practice of the Institutions and the Member States.

2.1. "United in Diversity": The Configurations of the Council of Ministers

One of the *raisons d'être* of the Constitution is the need for a better separation of the legislative and judicial functions. According to the federalist vision of Europe, the solution is simple: taking the German model as an example, the Council of Ministers would be one of two legislative organs (together with the European Parliament) and could adopt "delegated regulations" (i.e., regulations supplementing or amending non-essential elements of European laws or framework laws). However, what is valid for a federal State is not necessarily valid for a Union of sovereign States, in which the Council of Ministers also has other functions, i.e., the adoption of broad policy orientations (essentially attributed in the Convention's text to the European Council) and the coordination of policies in terms of both planning and execution. Certain members of the Convention sought to establish a clear separation between a "legislative Council" and an "executive Council". However, this idea was rejected by other members who preferred to maintain the Council's "unity".

This issue was directly tied to that of the Presidency. In the system established by the Treaties of Rome and Maastricht, the Member State occupying the Presidency is responsible, during a six-month period, for managing all the meetings of the Council at all levels, including those of: the European Council (where the relevant head of State or government presides); the Council of Ministers (relevant minister corresponding to the sector being discussed, whether it be agriculture, finance, etc.); and the Committee of Permanent Representatives, or "Coreper" (relevant ambassador or deputy ambassador to the Union). The Member State occupying the Presidency also manages the working groups (composed of high-level civil servants from national ministries or from the permanent representations located in Brussels) that negotiate the texts that Coreper or the Council of Ministers must approve.

This system of a rotating Presidency has a dual advantage. On the one hand, during the six months in which it holds the Presidency, the government and the administration of the Member State in question are obliged to take account of the general interests of the Union and the Community and gain intensive experience and knowledge as to how these two entities function. On the other hand, the fact that the Presidency rotates every six months avoids a situation in which the Member State abuses the post by imposing its own agenda – which could easily lead to a series of reprisals on the part of the other Member States once they take the helm. However, despite these advantages, the system is complex and barely comprehensible to the Union's citizens and to the rest of the world. Furthermore, the Presidency is extremely costly in terms of human resources for the Member State in charge. Finally, the advantages diminish as the number of Member States grows. Until 1973, a given Member State held the Presidency every three years. From 1986 to 1994, the frequency had dropped to one Presidency every six years. And under the regime in effect since 2004, each Member State must wait twelve and a half years between turns!

The creation by the Convention of a permanent Presidency of the European Council and of a Union Minister of Foreign Affairs, without rendering the system any simpler, at least makes it more comprehensible. The Constitution leaves it for the Council to find a solution which best reconciles the benefits of the rotation system with its costs: much as it had with respect to the composition of the Commission, the IGC retreated from the Convention's proposal concerning the rotating Presidency of the Council of Ministers (summarised in the table at page 132). First of all, the IGC jettisoned the idea of establishing a Legislative Council to distinguish between the Council's legislative and non-legislative activities. In addition, rather than fixing the modalities of the Presidency in the Constitution itself, the IGC adopted a Declaration incorporating a *Draft European decision of the European Council on the exercise of the Presidency of the Council* (see page 135). This draft European decision maintains the principle that the Foreign Minister will preside over the Foreign Affairs Council for a term of five years. However, in other respects it essentially returns to the *status quo ante*, including the traditional six-month Presidency corresponding to the Council's other configurations (which are to be enumerated by the European Council in a separate decision). Although the IGC was not prepared to go as far as the Convention, the draft decision would also permit the European Council to decide by qualified majority to modify this system should it prove inadequate to guarantee the proper functioning of the Council.

In addition to its uniquely structured Presidency, the Foreign Affairs Council stands out in the sense that it will be supported by a European External Action Service, the development of which is likely to facilitate a more solid common foreign policy. However, the role of this new diplomatic corps will depend greatly on the capacity of the Foreign Minister, as a *primus inter pares*, to treat the ministers of the Member States, particularly those most attached to their own diplomatic traditions, as equals.

With the system proposed by the Convention, the Ministers of European Affairs, who will sit on the General Affairs Council, would have been vested with greater authority in the context of their national governments. This could have contributed, on the one hand, to an improvement of national coordination mechanisms regarding European affairs and, on the other hand, to better visibility with respect to European policies in national debates, whether in the national parliament or before the media. It would also have been more difficult for governments to use Europe as a scapegoat by blaming "Brussels" for decisions made in reality by the national governments themselves.

The number of the other configurations will depend in part on reasons of substance, such as the necessity of specialised Councils. The draft European decision annexed to the Constitution makes it possible for groups of three Member States to share certain Council Presidencies among them, for example the Presidency of the Eurogroup. Some configurations may want to meet on a frequent basis while others may prefer to meet only once or twice a year.

The impact of this new system on the respective services of the Commission, the European Parliament and the Council of Ministers is impossible to predict. The possible reinforcement of the administration of the Council could have led to competition with that of the Commission, and the Member States know only too well the dangers of rivalry among administrative services.

Configurations of the Council of Ministers:
Comparison of the Convention's text and the Constitution

Text proposed by the Convention (Article 23)	Text of the Constitution (Article I-24)
1. [*The Legislative and General Affairs Council*] shall ensure consistency in the work of the Council of Ministers.	1. The Council shall meet in different configurations.
When it acts in its General Affairs function, it shall, in liaison with the Commission, prepare, and ensure follow-up to, meetings of the European Council.	2. The General Affairs Council shall ensure consistency in the work of the different Council configurations.
[*When it acts in its legislative function, the Council of Ministers shall consider and, jointly with the European Parliament, enact European laws and European framework laws, in accordance with the provisions of the Constitution. In this function, each Member State's representation shall include one or two representatives at ministerial level with relevant expertise, reflecting the business on the agenda of the Council of Ministers.*]	It shall prepare and ensure the follow-up to meetings of the European Council, in liaison with the President of the European Council and the Commission.

Configurations of the Council of Ministers:
Comparison of the Convention's text and the Constitution (Cont'd)

Text proposed by the Convention (Article 23)	Text of the Constitution (Article I-24)
2. The Foreign Affairs Council shall, on the basis of strategic guidelines laid down by the European Council, flesh out the Union's external policies, and ensure that its actions are consistent. It shall be chaired by the Union Minister for Foreign Affairs.	3. The Foreign Affairs Council shall elaborate the Union's external action on the basis of strategic guidelines laid down by the European Council and ensure that the Union's action is consistent.
3. The European Council shall adopt a European decision establishing further formations in which the Council of Ministers may meet.	4. The European Council shall adopt by a qualified majority a European decision establishing the list of other Council configurations.
(*cf.* Article III-247)	5. A Committee of Permanent Representatives of the Governments of the Member States shall be responsible for preparing the work of the Council.
(*cf.* Article I-49(2) : The European Parliament shall meet in public, as shall the Council of Ministers when examining and adopting a legislative proposal.)	6. The Council shall meet in public when it deliberates and votes on a draft legislative act. To this end, each Council meeting shall be divided into two parts, dealing respectively with deliberations on Union legislative acts and non-legislative activities.
4. The Presidency of Council of Ministers formations, other than that of Foreign Affairs, shall be held by Member State representatives within the Council of Ministers on the basis of equal rotation for periods of at least a year. The European Council shall adopt a European decision establishing the rules of such rotation, taking into account European political and geographical balance and the diversity of Member States.	7. The Presidency of Council configurations, other than that of Foreign Affairs, shall be held by Member State representatives in the Council on the basis of equal rotation, in accordance with the conditions established by a European decision of the European Council. The European Council shall act by a qualified majority.

Note: in the left-hand column, the text in italics was deleted by the IGC. In the right-hand column, the underlined text indicates a modification made by the IGC to the system proposed by the Convention.

Convention's Proposal Regarding the Rotating Presidency of the Council
(With Hypothetical Configurations Based on Certain Sectoral Portfolios)

Hypothetical configuration	Members	Presidency	Term	Meetings	Functions
European Council	Council President + 25 heads of State and government	Council President	2.5 years (renewable once)	4 times per year + extraordinary meetings	General political directions and priorities; decisions provided for in the Constitution

133

Convention's Proposal Regarding the Rotating Presidency of the Council
(With Hypothetical Configurations Based on Certain Sectoral Portfolios) (Cont'd)

Hypothetical configuration	Members	Presidency	Term	Meetings	Functions
Foreign Affairs Council	Union Minister for Foreign Affairs + 25 Foreign Ministers	Union Minister for Foreign Affairs	5 years	Every 3 weeks?	Decisions in the area of CFSP; adoption of mandates authorising the Commission to negotiate international treaties (trade, environment, etc.)
General Affairs Council	25 Ministers of European Affairs	Ministers of European Affairs from States A, B and C	A 6 months B 6 months C 6 months	Every 3 weeks?	General directions to Coreper; Decisions in cases unresolved by other configurations of the Council
Economic and Financial Affairs Council (?)	25 Ministers of the Economy and Finance	Ministers of Economy and Finance from States D, E and F	A 6 months B 6 months C 6 months	Every 5 weeks?	European decisions, recommendations and opinions in the area of economic and monetary policy
Agriculture Council (?)	25 Ministers of Agriculture	Ministers of Agriculture from States G, H and I	A 6 months B 6 months C 6 months	Every 6 weeks?	European decisions (management of agricultural markets)
Justice and Home Affairs Council (?)	25 Ministers of Justice or Internal Affairs	Ministers of Justice or Internal Affairs from States J, K and L	A 6 months B 6 months C 6 months	Every 8 weeks?	Decides orientations for the preparation of common legislation
Research Council (?)	25 Ministers of Research	Ministers of Research from States M, N and O	A 6 months B 6 months C 6 months	Every 3 months?	Decisions on the execution of research programmes
Employment and Labour Council (?)	25 Ministers of Employment	Ministers of Employment from States P, Q and R	A 6 months B 6 months C 6 months	Every 3 months?	Comparisons of employment and labour policies; establishment of objectives in the area of unemployment

Draft European Decision of the European Council
on the Exercise of the Presidency of the Council

ARTICLE 1

1. The Presidency of the Council, with the exception of the Foreign Affairs configuration, shall be held by pre-established groups of three Member States for a period of 18 months. The groups shall be made up on a basis of equal rotation among the Member States, taking into account their diversity and geographical balance within the Union.

2. Each member of the group shall in turn chair for a six-month period all configurations of the Council, with the exception of the Foreign Affairs configuration. The other members of the group shall assist the Chair in all its responsibilities on the basis of a common programme. Members of the team may decide alternative arrangements among themselves.

ARTICLE 2

The Committee of Permanent Representatives of the Governments of the Member States shall be chaired by a representative of the Member State chairing the General Affairs Council.

The Chair of the Political and Security Committee shall be held by a representative of the Union Minister for Foreign Affairs.

The chair of the preparatory bodies of the various Council configurations, with the exception of the Foreign Affairs configuration, shall fall to the member of the group chairing the relevant configuration, unless decided otherwise in accordance with Article 4.

ARTICLE 3

The General Affairs Council shall ensure consistency and continuity in the work of the different Council configurations in the framework of multiannual programmes in cooperation with the Commission. The Member States holding the Presidency shall take all necessary measures for the organisation and smooth operation of the Council's work, with the assistance of the General Secretariat of the Council.

ARTICLE 4

The Council shall adopt a European decision establishing the measures for the implementation of this decision.

2.2. Alarm Bells for the Parliaments

When the European Council decided in 1985 that it was imperative to complete the internal market by January of 1992, the Community's pace of legislative activity quickened to an astonishing degree. To achieve a greater harmonisation among national legislation, the programme envisaged three hundred new measures covering technical, security and public health standards among many others. The point of the exercise was to address the divergent rules applying in the various Member States which prevented consumers from enjoying the benefits of a market potentially larger than that in the United States.

During the run-up to 1992, national parliaments were therefore faced with an accelerated influx of Directives from Brussels, which they were then obliged to transpose into national law. It did not take them long to realise that the European institutional system was progressively depriving them of their traditional margin of manoeuvre as legislators. Some parliamentarians understood that their waning influence was being regained indirectly through their respective governments due to the participation of the latter in the Council of Ministers. However, others believed that their powers were in fact being sapped to the advantage of the Commission.

Since then, all of the IGCs have sought to create mechanisms to enhance the role of national parliaments in European decision making. The great novelty of the European Convention is that, for the first time, the parliaments had a voice, whereas with the IGC system they were (at best) simply kept informed by their respective governments. And with half of the Convention populated with national parliamentarians, this voice was not a soft one.

That is precisely why it is interesting to see that the Convention's text does not distort the general architecture of the relationships between national parliaments and the European Institutions but rather limits itself to two noteworthy modifications. These are embodied in the two protocols adopted by the Convention at the recommendation of Working Groups I and IV, i.e., the *Protocol on the role of national Parliaments in the European Union* and the *Protocol on the application of the principles of subsidiarity and proportionality*. The new provisions contained in these instruments may create very interesting possibilities for the national parliaments, and may provide means by which to regain some of the influence they have lost as a result of not only the process of European integration but also the monopoly over legislative initiative enjoyed by the governments and administrations of most Member States.

The first innovation may seemingly appear to be of minor importance. At present, national parliaments do receive copies of the legislative proposals made by the Commission to the Council and the European Parliament, but only indirectly through the channel of their respective governments. Each Member State's permanent representation in Brussels transmits the proposals to its central administration, which in turn furnishes a copy to the relevant parliamentary body. By contrast, the two Protocols to the Constitution referred to above oblige the Commission directly to transmit to the national parliaments all consultation documents (i.e., green and white papers and communications) upon publication and all legislative proposals at the same time as they are submitted to the Council and the European Parliament. In this era of electronic communications, the new dispositions might not appear as significant as they would have been prior to the mid-1990s, when transmission of proposals to parliaments was much more time-consuming. However, the most important aspect of the Commission's new information obligation is that national ministers and civil servants will no longer be in a position to delay the transmission of these documents to the parliaments. Even more importantly, parliaments will no longer be able to complain that such delays prevent them from doing their work.

The second innovation is complementary to the information obligation described above. Often called an *early warning* system, a Protocol to the Constitution allows the national parliaments to review the legislative proposals of the Institutions and to request that they be revised if they consider such proposals to be deficient from the point of view of subsidiarity or proportionality. Essentially, if at least a third of the national parliaments (or, in the case of certain proposals in the field of freedom, security and justice, at least a quarter of them) submit, within six weeks, reasoned opinions concluding that a proposal fails to comply with those principles, the draft legislation must be reviewed. The Institution in question may decide to maintain, amend or withdraw the draft measure, and must give reasons for its decision. The Protocol further provides that the Court of Justice may hear cases brought against the Institutions for infringement of the subsidiarity principle by a Member State not only on its own behalf but also on behalf of its parliament or one of its parliamentary chambers. Finally, the Protocol makes it possible for the Committee of the Regions to bring such actions provided the Constitution requires the Institutions to consult the Committee prior to the adoption of the legislative act in question.

There is little point in lingering over the rather complex details of the early warning system, as it is not designed to engender quarrels of procedure between the national parliaments and the European Institutions. What matters, first of all, is that the simple existence of this novel mechanism should encourage the Institutions and national governments to engage in more meaningful consultation with national parliaments before it is too late for the latter to have any impact. Furthermore and even more importantly, the early warning system should serve to induce the parliaments to become more interested and more closely involved in the decision-making process of the Institutions and to organise themselves (both internally and, to some degree, across national boundaries) accordingly.

3. Less Simple Than It Seems

3.1. Legal Personality: The Tree Hiding the Forest

The decisive step toward the adoption of a draft Constitution – and not simply a report on the Convention's proceedings – was taken in September of 2002 within Working Group III, chaired by Giuliano Amato. The working group was charged with the task of studying a question which superficially appears both technical and boring.

In 1951 and 1957, the Treaties establishing the Coal and Steel Community, the European Atomic Energy Community (Euratom) and the European Economic Community provided explicitly that each Community "shall have legal personality". This comes as no surprise, considering that analogous provisions are found in any treaty establishing an international organisation, whether it be, for example, the United Nations or the Universal Postal Union. Briefly stated, the fact that the European Community has a legal personality means that it may enter into treaties with third countries or international organisations, conclude contracts, and bring legal actions in the courts of the Member States.

However, no such provision declaring a legal personality was incorporated in the Treaty of Maastricht of 1992, due in particular to the British government's hesitations with respect to the advance of European integration. Since then, specialists in international law have debated whether the Union nevertheless has a *de facto* legal personality on the basis of its activities as an international organisation.

Following a typically functionalist means of reasoning, Working Group III adopted a position in favour of a series of options. These options bore a logical connection, but at the same time no link of the chain followed necessarily from the preceding one:

- Should the Union have an explicit legal personality? Yes – it is totally illogical that the Union is not specifically endowed with a legal personality while the Communities are.
- Is it justified to maintain different organisations with different names but having the same Institutions and the same Member States? No – the system is pointlessly complex and difficult to explain, both to the citizens of the Union and to the rest of the world.
- If it is decided that the Union and the Communities should be replaced by a single organisation, does it make sense to maintain different Treaties governing distinct activities? No – the resulting framework would be too complicated and difficult to read.
- If it is decided that the Treaty on European Union and the EC Treaty should be replaced with a single Treaty, why not give it the title "*Constitution for Europe*"? Indeed, why not? . . .

It was affirmed many times, both in the debates of the Convention and by numerous commentators, that establishing an explicit legal personality would enable it to participate in certain international organisations, including for example the United Nations. This assertion, while not altogether mistaken, should be qualified. As the European Union is not a sovereign State, it can only become a member of an international organisation if the charter of the organisation allow non-States to join. If membership is limited to States only – as in the case of the UN – a consensus of the contracting States would be required to change the charter in order to open the door to the Union. In this connection, it should be pointed out that the European Community already belongs to a certain number of international organisations, including in particular the World Trade Organisation. Since the legal personality of the Community is to be superseded by that of the Union once the Constitution is ratified, the Union will accordingly succeed the Community as a member of such organisations.

Step by step, the issue of legal personality allowed the Convention to take a series of decisions leading it toward a reinforcement of the constitutional character of the Union. One of the most significant instances of this process was the decision to reel in the three pillars and to place them all within a single Treaty.

3.2. The Pillars are Gone, the Distinctions Remain

When the Member States agreed in 1985 to institutionalise cooperation in the field of foreign policy, they deliberately kept decision making in this field beyond the reach of the Community method. The Member States were keen to avoid involving the Commission and the European Parliament in the development and management of a policy field so closely connected to their sovereignty. In 1992, when institutionalising cooperation in judicial and police matters (i.e., "Justice and Home Affairs"), similar sensitivities led the Member States to hold this field separate from the Community as well.

This explains why the Maastricht Treaty consisted of three essential elements, in particular:

– a series of reforms concerning the Community, among which the most important were the establishment of the Economic and Monetary Union and the transformation of the European Economic Community into the European Community as a consequence of the introduction of a European citizenship and numerous new legal bases in areas stretching ever father away from economic matters;
– the shift from "cooperation in the sphere of foreign policy" to a Common Foreign and Security Policy (CFSP); and
– the establishment of cooperation in Justice and Home Affairs.

With the exception of the Court of Justice, all of the Institutions played a role in all three of these fields, i.e., in the CFSP and in Justice and Home Affairs as well as in the European Communities with their diverse policy areas. However, the procedures used and the powers at the Institutions' disposal differed according to the field concerned. From this was born the idea of representing the EU as a kind of ancient temple, with a common base (the Institutions), three pillars (the Communities, the CFSP and Justice and Home Affairs – which became the "Area of Freedom, Security and Justice" with the Treaty of Amsterdam), and a pediment on which the word "citizenship" is inscribed. The architectural talents of the national governments at the IGC were questionable from the outset: leaving aside the fact that the Union's pillars are of remarkably varying widths, the only temples that have just three pillars are decrepit and lay in ruins.

The pillar structure defied any simple explanation of the organisation and functioning of the EU. Worse, it caused numerous legal and technical problems and led to friction among the Institutions. However, during the IGCs of Maastricht, Amsterdam and Nice the national governments have shown themselves to be highly conservative, avoiding changes to the settlement already reached in connection with the Single European Act, when intergovernmental cooperation was institutionalised without integrating it as part of the Community.

In principle, the abolition of the pillars should mean that the same procedures and same legal instruments apply in all fields of Union law. At the same time, the jurisdiction of the Court of Justice (no longer "of the European *Community*" but "of the European *Union*") is further expanded so that in principle it may give rulings in all of those fields. Any derogation from the common procedures requires a specific provision to that effect in the Constitution and must be justified by appropriate political or technical reasons.

Deciding to simplify the Union by scrapping the pillar structure is one of the great accomplishments of the Convention. Indeed, unifying the Union's policies within a single text has eliminated many problems linked directly to the complexity of the now-condemned architecture. However, traces from the old system are reflected in a variability in the powers and procedures in certain fields: the balance of power among the European Parliament, the Council, the Commission and the Member States is not quite the same in the field of the CFSP or the Area of Freedom, Security and Justice as it is in other fields. But then, even at the national level, the balance of institutional power shifts according to whether a decision falls within the sphere of foreign or internal policy.

In this regard, one of the most visible differences concerns decision making within the Council of Ministers. Whereas, with respect to internal matters, voting by qualified majority is the rule and unanimity the exception, in the field of the CFSP decisions are generally adopted by unanimous vote. The use of qualified majority voting is limited to certain technical decisions used for the implementation of policy.

There are various divergent opinions concerning the need to apply qualified majority voting in the field of foreign policy. In any case, it should not be forgotten that, in times of crisis, the power to make foreign policy decisions of any Sate is concentrated in the hands of an extremely limited number of persons: in general, the head of State, the head of government and the Foreign Minister. Even if qualified majority voting were to apply to foreign policy decisions, it would still be necessary (in the present Union of 25 Member States) for at least fifteen Foreign Ministers to agree on a course of action. Furthermore, these ministers would have to justify their decisions before their respective governments and parliaments.

3.3. Categorising Competences

Beginning in 1987, as efforts to complete the internal market were stepped up dramatically, the Community began to give off the impression that it was dramatically increasing the extent of its intervention in numerous fields while progressively depriving national parliaments – and especially regions with legislative powers such as the German *Länder* – of their influence and autonomy. This development may be explained by two principal underlying causes.

The first is directly linked to the concept of the internal market, according to which national rules restricting the free movement of goods, services, workers and capital are in principle forbidden. The goal of eliminating direct and indirect barriers to such cross-border trade has indeed frequently led the Community to adopt common, "harmonising" rules applicable to all the Member States. In the absence of such common rules, Member States often found themselves condemned for violating the EC Treaty by maintaining trade barriers in legal actions brought by citizens or enterprises. Although this did not create new competences for the Union, it did make the Community's competence to intervene in order to promote the internal market increasingly obvious.

The second reason why the powers of parliaments and regional authorities were slipping away is that the governments of the Member States often found it expedient to favour intervention by the Community. At times this was because governments felt that action at national level would be inadequate, particularly (but not only) in the case the smaller Member States. At other times, national governments simply lacked the courage to pursue, at the national level, reforms which they knew to be unpopular; they preferred to be able to explain to the public that such reforms had been imposed on them by Europe.

Paradoxically, beginning with the Single European Act it has essentially been through the revision of the Treaties – and hence in a highly visible manner – that the competences of the Community and the Union have been expanded, whereas prior to 1985 important new competences had passed quietly and undetected. During that era, maximum use was made of the "flexibility clause", i.e., Article 308 (ex-Article 235) of the EC Treaty, which grants the Community certain "implied powers": this is how, particularly with the involvement of Denmark and the UK following their accession in 1973, the Community began taking action notably in the areas of regional and environmental policy.

This apparently indiscriminate expansion of competences provoked increasingly numerous demands that either certain common policies be "re-nationalised", or that the creeping advance of competences be halted, or at least that it be clarified "who does what" in Europe. It was therefore little surprise that voices from many quarters were calling on the Convention to establish a "catalogue of competences" to identify how powers are shared between the European and national levels.

However, an analysis of these various demands reveals their contradictions. Some called on the Community to abandon this or that policy while others advocated, to the contrary, a reinforcement of the Community's competence in the same field: the nature of the demand depended on the burdens or benefits that would accrue at the national level. A typical case was the policy on structural funds. The point of view of a rather wealthy German *Land* such as Baden-Württemberg is necessarily opposed to that of a relatively poor Spanish region such as Andalusia. Meanwhile, the Convention debates showed that citizens had high expectations that Europe would help them solve the problems of daily life, even in fields where the Union has neither competence nor means of action.

In federal States, constitutions generally contain a catalogue of competences making it possible to establish the respective responsibilities of the federation and its members. However, these catalogues are either so concise that, like the US Constitution, they paint only a very partial picture of reality – or else they are finely detailed to the point of being unreadable, as in the case of Austria, for example. Furthermore, as the means of public action are developed, other instruments based not on law but on other considerations become increasingly important, including in particular financial priorities. Yet federal constitutions generally do not go beyond enumerating legislative powers.

The Convention was thus faced with the impossible task of squaring the circle, and its solution reflects the complexity of the problem: to appreciate all the dimensions of the division of competences within the Union, it is not enough merely to read the Articles contained in Title III of Part I, which is dedicated to this theme. In addition to understanding the general framework laid down in Title III, one must refer to the more detailed provisions of Part III in order to grasp who does what and how. Still, the Constitution is unquestionably an important step forward in that, for the first time since 1986, a serious attempt has been made to articulate a coherent system. By contrast, the texts adopted by past IGCs have been, at best, documents written by experts for experts.

While it is impractical to include in this book a comprehensive table covering all of the various corresponding legal bases, a more modest table can be constructed which sets forth a panorama of competences drawn from Articles I-12 to I-17 of the Constitution (see below).

General Framework of the Allocation of Competences
among the Union and the Member States
(Articles I-12 to I-17 of the Constitution)

Category	Definition	Fields
1. Exclusive competences of the Union	*Article I-12(1):* When the Constitution confers on the Union exclusive competence in a specific area, only the Union may legislate and adopt legally binding acts, the Member States being able to do so themselves only if so empowered by the Union or for the implementation of Union acts.	*Article I-13:* – Customs union – Competition rules where they are necessary for the functioning of the internal market – Monetary policy for Member States whose currency is the euro – Conservation of marine biological resources under the common fisheries policy – Common commercial policy

General Framework of the Allocation of Competences
among the Union and the Member States
(Articles I-12 to I-17 of the Constitution) (Cont'd)

Category	Definition	Fields
		– The conclusion of inter-national agreements where: provided for in a legislative act; necessary to enable the Union to exercise its internal competence; or its conclusion may affect common rules or alter their scope.
2. Shared competences (possible pre-emption)	*Article I-12(2)*: When the Constitution confers on the Union a competence shared with the Member States in a specific area, the Union and the Member States may legislate and adopt legally binding acts in that area. The Member States shall exercise their competence to the extent that the Union has not exercised, or has decided to cease exercising, its competence.	*Article I-14*: – Internal market – Social policy, for the aspects defined in Part III – Economic, social and territorial cohesion – Agriculture and fisheries, excluding the conservation of marine biological resources – Environment – Consumer protection – Transport – Trans-European networks – Energy – Area of freedom, security and justice – Common safety concerns in public health matters, for the aspects defined in Part III – Residual fields not covered by categories 1, 2 *bis*, 3 or 3 *bis*
2 *bis*. Shared competences (no pre-emption)	*Articles I-14(3), I-14(4)*: The Union shall have competence to carry out activities, in particular to define and implement programmes (and in the case of development cooperation and humanitarian aid to conduct a common policy); however, the exercise of that competence shall not result in Member States being prevented from exercising theirs.	*Articles I-14(3), I-14(4)*: – Research, technological development and space – Development cooperation and humanitarian aid
3. Areas of supporting, coordinating or complementary	*Article I-12(5)*: In certain areas and under the conditions laid down in the Constitution, the Union shall have competence to carry out actions	*Article I-15 (economic and employment policies)*: The Member States shall coordinate their economic and

*General Framework of the Allocation of Competences
among the Union and the Member States
(Articles I-12 to I-17 of the Constitution)* (Cont'd)

Category	Definition	Fields
action	to support, coordinate or supplement the actions of the Member States, without superseding their competence in these areas.	employment policies within the Union. The Union shall take measures to ensure this, in particular by adopting guidelines.
	Legally binding acts of the Union adopted on the basis of the provisions in Part III relating to these areas shall not entail harmonisation of Member States' laws or regulations.	*Article I-17 (other fields)*: – The protection and improvement of human health – Industry – Culture – Tourism – Education, youth, sport and vocational training – Civil protection – Administrative cooperation
3 *bis*. Coordinatng or complementary action in the field of the CFSP	*Article I-16(2)*: Member States shall actively and unreservedly support the Union's common foreign and security policy in a spirit of loyalty and mutual solidarity and shall comply with the Union's action in this area. They shall refrain from action contrary to the Union's interests or likely to impair its effectiveness.	*Article I-16*: All areas of foreign policy and all questions relating to the Union's security, including the progressive framing of a common defence policy that might lead to a common defence.

Professors of European Union law can breathe a sigh of satisfaction: they have plenty of raw material with which to demonstrate their originality, and they will be able to develop their own stylised competence typologies. They will then have to explain the exact scope of the principles recalled by Articles I-6 and I-11, which attempts to formulate certain well established notions, some of which had heretofore appeared only in the jurisprudence of the Court of Justice, such as the principle of primacy. They will furthermore have to sound out the possibilities and the limits of the above-mentioned flexibility clause (Article I-18), comparing them to the possibility of "enhanced cooperation" among a limited number of Member States (Article I-44).

3.4. Simplification of Instruments and Procedures

Another simplification exercise awaited the Convention. It already takes a good deal of time to explain the differences between *directives, regulations, decisions, recommendations* and *opinions* to citizens accustomed to hearing about laws, decrees and regulations under their national laws. The authors of the Treaty of Rome had strictly defined these instruments, specifying that only the first three were legally binding (Article 249 EC; ex-Article 189). However, since then the Council of Ministers, the Commission and the European Parliament progressively multiplied the types of instruments they used, and the IGCs added many others, especially in connection with the second and third pillars but also for fields within the ambit of the Community. Eventually it became practically impossible to compile an exhaustive list of these sundry instruments, let alone define them all.

Moreover, the name of a given instrument offers no hint as to the procedure used for its adoption. To illustrate, a directive in principle gives Member States relatively precise, binding instructions as to the result to be achieved but leaves to national authorities the choice of the forms and methods (such as laws and decrees) to be used when transposing the principles of the directive at the national level (Article 249 EC; ex-Article 189). But directives can be adopted, depending on the circumstances, by the Council, by the Commission, or jointly by the Council and the Parliament. In each case it is necessary to refer to the specific legal base of the Treaty in order to know what kind of directive is at issue.

The Constitution seeks to introduce some order and eliminate the confusion that arises from the myriad of possible procedures under the current system. The approach embraced by the Constitution more closely resembles the hierarchical system of laws and regulations to which the citizens of the Member States are accustomed. The system of the Union remains comparatively complex, but to some degree this seems inevitable. On the one hand, since the Union is not a State its procedures cannot perfectly replicate customary national procedures. On the other hand, the acute concern of certain governments for the protection of national interests and prerogatives leads them in some cases to confer very distinctive powers on the Council.

The Legal Acts of the Union (Article I-33 of the Constitution)

Category	Procedure for adoption	Effect	Implementing measures	Derogation procedures
European law	Proposed by the Commission. Majority vote by the Parliament and QMV by the Council of Ministers.	Generally applicable. Binding in its entirety and directly applicable in all Member States.	If necessary, delegated regulations or decisions by the Institutions.	Unanimous vote of the Council. Simple opinion of the Parliament. Any derogation must be stipulated in the procedure described in Part III.

The Legal Acts of the Union (Article I-33 of the Constitution) (Cont'd)

Category	Procedure for adoption	Effect	Implementing measures	Derogation procedures
European framework law	Proposed by the Commission. Majority vote by the Parliament and QMV by the Council of Ministers.	Binding and must be transposed into national law by the Member States to which it is addressed.	Laws and decrees of the Member States.	Unanimous vote of the Council. Simple opinion of the Parliament. Any derogation must be stipulated in the procedure described in Part III.
European regulation	Proposed by the Commission. QMV by the Council of Ministers (unless unanimous vote is required).	Generally applicable and used for implementing European laws and framework laws and certain provisions of the Constitution. It is either binding in its entirety and directly applicable in all the Member States or binding and must be transposed into national law by the Member States to which it is addressed.	Delegated regulations or decisions of the Institutions. Laws and decrees of the Member States.	Regulations adopted by the Commission or by the European Central Bank.
Delegated regulation	A European law or framework law delegates to the Commission the power to adopt delegated European regulations to supplement or amend non-essential elements of the law or framework law.	Generally applicable provided the Parliament and the Council of Ministers do not object.	Decisions by the Commission. By way of exception, acts of the Member States.	n/a
European decision	(i) QMV or unanimous vote by the European Council; (ii) Proposed by the Commission. QMV by the Council of	Binding in its entirety. If addressees are specified (as is nearly always the case), it is binding only on them.	n/a	Certain decisions are provided for in the Constitution (particularly those of the European Council). In other cases, European decisions may be

146

The Legal Acts of the Union (Article I-33 of the Constitution) (Cont'd)

Category	Procedure for adoption	Effect	Implementing measures	Derogation procedures
	Ministers; (iii) Decisions taken by the managing organs of the Institutions or bodies of the Union, or by the European Central Bank.			taken in order to implement European laws or regulations.

In order for the system to be truly complete, the Court of Justice will have to develop a set of principles designed to verify, at one level, the conformity of European laws and regulations with the Constitution, and then, at a subsidiary level, the conformity of delegated regulations and European decisions with European laws and regulations. With regard to judicial review of certain acts of the Union, an important new development has also emerged, although it takes a specialist experienced in the procedures of the European Courts to notice what the Convention has done. According to Article III-365(4) of the Constitution, any person may bring proceedings "against a regulatory act which is of direct concern to him or her and does not entail implementing measures". This new formulation entails a subtle but significant relaxation of the conditions in which a person may challenge a "regulatory act", i.e., an act that is not a European law or framework law but which nevertheless applies to a broad class of people, provided it does not require implementing measures by the authorities at either national or Union level.

3.5. . . . And Many Other Innovations . . .

The Constitution was conceived with the idea that, after having read the first two parts of it, the citizen should have a sufficiently clear notion of what the Union is and what it does. The text favourably compares to many other national constitutions, including both older texts such as that of the United States, and newer ones such as those in Finland, the countries of Central and Eastern Europe, and The Netherlands.

Furthermore, many of the provisions of the European Constitution are formulated in a general manner, similar to the style of a national constitution. However, the principle of "conferral", according to which the Member States attribute competences to the Union (as they did previously to the Communities) to attain common objectives, requires a text with greater precision for those that must apply it, namely, the European Parliament, the Member States, the European

Council and the Council of Ministers, the Court of Justice, judges, lawyers, civil servants, professors and students. In order to apply the Constitution's provisions correctly, they will have to refer continuously to Part III in order to verify the details of the mechanisms of which they avail themselves. In particular they will have to be attentive to whether they are navigating in a field where the general rules apply, or whether they are instead in a less trodden zone where the exception confirms the rule. As they weave in and out of the terrain, numerous other innovations introduced by the Convention will become apparent.

Some of the Convention's innovations are indeed quite evident and can be discerned on a first reading of the Convention's text or of the Constitution. Among many other novelties, the following in particular may be mentioned:

- an ordinary legislative procedure (Article III-396) which is clear and balanced and which replaces the *Snakes and Ladders* game known as the "co-decision procedure". The central role of this procedure demonstrates the value of having so many experienced parliamentarians among the members of the Convention, including the Presidency.

- the possibility of a *citizens' initiative* (Article I-47(4)) by which a group of a million citizens or more representing several Member States may invite the Commission to submit proposals for the purpose of implementing the Constitution. This tentative but highly symbolic experiment with direct democracy represents a constructive compromise between the federalist vision and the Community method.

- certain new legal bases for matters that had not previously fallen within the competences of the Union or the Community (tourism, Article III-281; civil protection, Article III-284; administrative cooperation, Article III-285). These new competences are the latest tiny steps marching to the functionalist drumbeat.

- the first foundations for a common defence policy (Articles III-309 to III-312). The IGC not only maintained the Convention's proposals but strengthened them to a certain degree.

- an allusion to the "open method of coordination" (Article I-15). As the open method of coordination allows Member States to discuss different national solutions while sidestepping the Community method, it is a fundamentally intergovernmental mechanism. At the same time, it exposes certain policy regimes of the Member States to informal appraisal by the others.

- a significant enhancement of the possibilities of bringing legal actions before the Court of Justice (abolition of the pillars, which in particular brings most fields in the Area of Freedom, Security and Justice within the jurisdiction of the Court; the above-mentioned Article III-365(4) regarding challenges to regulatory acts; and the Protocol on the application of the principles of subsidiarity and proportionality, discussed earlier, which creates new means to challenge

legislation on subsidiarity grounds). These important developments all strengthen the Union's claim to be founded on the value of the rule of law.
- a re-definition of the Union's budgetary procedures (Articles III-403 to III-414). The enhanced powers of the Parliament in terms of budget approval signal a return to the roots of constitutionalism (reminiscent of the origins of the parliamentary systems in France and the UK).

But this cursory glance hardly does justice to the work of the Convention (as revised and in some respects improved by the IGC). Indeed, far from being a mere cut-and-paste exercise, the Constitution contains numerous and interesting minor innovations whose potential will only be revealed over time.

Given the conditions under which it was drafted and the more than 200 assembly members whose input it contains, the Constitution appears at this very early juncture to be extremely coherent, particularly in light of the concerns raised by the early drafts published between January and May of 2003. While no constitutional text is above reproach, this one is unquestionably more rich and coherent than the Treaties of Maastricht, Amsterdam and Nice.

The difficult tasks ahead will be losing the habit of saying "Community law" and – most terrifying of all – memorising the newly numbered Articles.

CHAPTER V

THE ROAD AHEAD

1. ENLARGEMENT: IS THE CONSTITUTION SUITABLE FOR A EUROPE OF 25+ MEMBER STATES?

To what does the European Union aspire? The debate on this theme which accompanied the first phase of the Convention, is in itself revealing in regard to the inherent difficulties in cooperation among Europeans.

In French, to ask, "What is the *finalité* of the Union?" is an elegant way to inquire: "What purpose does it serve?" However, when the term *finalité* was used by the English in the context of the same debate, it had at least two meanings that differed from the way the French understand it:

– What must the Union *be* in the end? A federal State, a confederation, an international organisation? Or perhaps, as Jacques Delors famously described it, an "unidentified political object"?
– What are Union's frontiers? Should it welcome Turkey? Should it exclude Russia? Etc.

The Convention certainly did not resolve such questions. In the first place, this was not its task. And indeed, sailing into those waters would have been the surest way for the Convention to run itself aground. The Constitution thus remains a Constitution for what a mathematician might call an "open set" (that is, a region without boundaries), not only with respect to its frontiers but also its form. It is neither a State, nor simply an international organisation, and still less a mere free trade zone.

1.1. Concurrent Undertakings: The Convention and Enlargement

Reading the text of the Convention, it may be wondered whether enlargement was really the *raison d'être* of the Laeken mandate or whether it was rather a pretext for reforms that were unavoidable. This is an insoluble question.

It is much more interesting to note that the Convention arrived at the right moment, neither too early nor too late. If the work had been carried out earlier, in particular during the IGCs at Amsterdam or Nice, the process would have totally excluded the representatives of all of the candidate States, or in other words nearly half of the countries likely to belong to the Union by 2010. From the time the Convention began its work in March of 2002, the date was sufficiently close to the conclusion of the Union's accession negotiations with the ten "first wave" candidate countries to make the members of the Convention feel obligated to listen to their new colleagues and to draw the interest of the latter in the Convention process.

The influence of the 78 representatives of the candidate countries in the outcome of that process is impossible to establish owing to the subtle alchemy of the Convention's consensus-based decision making. However, these representatives were present not only in plenary but also in the Praesidium and in all of the working groups and discussion circles. It is also interesting to note that they never took positions as a single bloc, although this would surely have been the case if they had perceived among the members of the Convention an East/West divide. In short, the representatives of the new Member States may lay the same claim to the Convention's text as may the members of the Convention representing the fifteen older ones. The IGC confirmed this impression: instead of seeking to assemble a bloc with the nine other new Member States, Poland chose instead to ally itself with Spain, the country most similar to it in terms of population size.

One glance at the figures (see below) shows that the double majority voting mechanism and a reduced college of Commissioners were reforms that had to be made sooner or later. At least in this regard, the enlargement of the Union changes things in an altogether obvious way. The Union will change in many other ways due to its new size; however, these changes will emerge in the *management* of the enterprise rather than in its constitutional structure, which simply has to be solid enough to withstand the turbulence.

List of Successive Enlargements

Date of Accession	Country	Population in 2004 (millions)
1952	Belgium	10.4
1952	France	59.6
1952	Germany	82.5
1952	Italy	57.3
1952	Luxembourg	0.4
1952	The Netherlands	16.2
1973	Denmark	5.4
1973	Ireland	4.0
1973	The United Kingdom	59.3
1981	Greece	11.0
1986	Portugal	10.4
1986	Spain	41.5
(1990)	(Reunification of Germany)	
1995	Austria	8.0
1995	Finland	5.2

List of Successive Enlargements (Cont'd)

Date of Accession	Country	Population in 2004 (millions)
1995	Sweden	8.9
2004	Cyprus	0.7
2004	Czech Republic	10.2
2004	Estonia	1.4
2004	Hungary	10.1
2004	Latvia	2.3
2004	Lithuania	3.4
2004	Malta	0.4
2004	Poland	38.2
2004	Slovak Republic	5.4
2004	Slovenia	2.0
2007 (?)	Bulgaria	8.0
2007 (?)	Romania	21.7
???	Croatia	4.4
???	Turkey	67.8
???	Albania	3.5
???	Bosnia-Herzegovina	4.0
???	Macedonia	2.1
???	Norway (?)	4.5
???	Switzerland (?)	7.4
???	Ukraine (?)	47.7
???	Etc.	

Sources: Eurostat yearbook 2004: The statistical guide to Europe for EEA countries; the European Commission's website for candidate countries; and http://www.populationdata.net for Albania, Bosnia-Herzegovina, Macedonia, Switzerland and Ukraine.

1.2. Wider versus Deeper?

Ever since de Gaulle's opposition in 1963 and again in 1967 to the accession of the UK to the European Community, many have repeatedly argued that the integration project must be consolidated and "deepened" before the Community – with the argument now applying to the Union – is expanded any further. Otherwise, it is argued, the process of enlargement will dilute the Community/Union to the point where it is little more than a free trade zone.

The events of 2002-04 demonstrate the opposite: the so-called fracture between "new" and "old" Europe, much discussed during the Iraq war, did not prevent the Convention from adopting its text by consensus, nor did it subsequently detain the IGC from approving it. Furthermore, the *acquis communautaire*, which is the foundation underlying the Union and which goes far beyond a free trade zone, was never called into question during the accession negotiations with the candidate countries from Central and Eastern Europe. These negotiations were concluded in March of 2003 without any attempts by the governments of either the candidate countries or the Member States to take advantage of the complexity of the negotiations in order to form coalitions of opportunity.

The Constitution is understandably silent regarding the European Economic Area (EEA). The EEA was established in 1994 by the EEA Agreement, a treaty signed by the twelve Member States belonging to the EU at that time and by six of the seven non-EU countries belonging to the European Free Trade Association (EFTA), including Austria, Finland and Sweden, who joined the Union in 1995. This agreement unites all of its eighteen member countries in an internal market subject more or less to the same internal market rules, and certain related policies, that apply to the Community. Although the accession of Austria, Finland and Sweden diminished its relative importance, the EEA continues to exist and links all of the Member States of the Union to Iceland, Liechtenstein and Norway. It should also be recalled that a number of specific agreements link the Community with Switzerland as well as Andorra, Monaco and San Marino. The Constitution alludes to these special relationships in Article I-57, *The Union and its neighbours*.

The more the "Treaty establishing a Constitution for Europe" transforms itself into a *Constitution* properly so called, the more the citizens of these countries closely linked to the Union will have cause to consider the implications of this process: what will happen to their independence if the vast majority of the economic legislation that applies within their borders is elaborated by the Institutions of the Union, in which their representatives do not participate?

2. RATIFICATION AND ENTRY INTO FORCE

The fact that the Constitution was signed by the heads of State and government in Rome on 29 October 2004 is not in itself sufficient to trigger the text's entry into force, as it must still be ratified by all of the Member States in accordance with their respective constitutional procedures. Experience with ratification of the previous Treaties teaches that this process is by no means guaranteed to be quick or easy.

The Penelope draft, prepared in December of 2003 at the behest of Commission President Prodi, incorporated a mechanism designed to overcome obstacles that could arise if the ratification process were held up by a particular Member State. According to this mechanism – inspired in part by the procedure used for ratifying the United States Constitution of 1787 – the new European Constitution would enter into force once three-fourths of the Member States had ratified it. Member States which by that point in time had failed to do so would be deemed to have opted out of the Union while remaining, however, a member of the EEA. In its legal formulation, the solution was as astute and elegant as it was fanciful. Indeed, it was obvious that this mechanism would not be acceptable for certain veteran Member States, notably Denmark and the UK, and still less so for the new Member States, who had just spent several years going through intensive reforms to qualify for membership in the Union. Furthermore, the Penelope draft rather arrogantly neglected to give the non-EU members of the EEA any say in the matter.

2.1. *Approval of the Citizens*

The constitutions of a certain number of Member States of the Union call for a popular referendum, under specified conditions, for the purpose of ratifying international treaties having implications for national sovereignty. By contrast, in other Member States the government may choose either to submit the question of ratification to a referendum or to limit the ratification process to a parliamentary vote. Finally, in some Member States the national constitution either does not permit referendums (as in Germany) or else does not permit the abrogation of treaties – in this case the abrogation of the Treaties of Rome and Maastricht – by way of a referendum procedure (as in Italy). Numerous voices were calling for a general referendum – to be held on the new Constitution in all the Member States – even before the Convention began its work. However, for reasons relating to the constitutional laws of most Member States, organising such a referendum would have required a great deal of time.

In the wake of the European Council in Thessaloniki in June of 2003, a group of Convention members proposed an alternative and more practicable solution. Indeed, at the Thessaloniki Council, the Italian representatives suggested that the Constitution could be signed on 9 May 2004, i.e., the anniversary of the Schuman Declaration and, more importantly, a day falling between 1 May – the date of accession for the ten new Member States – and 13 June, the date on which elections to the European Parliament were scheduled to begin. According to the proposal made by the group of Convention members, each Member State would have organised, contemporaneously with the European elections, either a parliamentary debate or a referendum on ratification of the Constitution. This would have been like felling two birds with one stone. On the one hand, it would have given the European elections the sense of a real contest, as the various parties could have taken the opportunity to present their favoured candidates for the post of President of the Commission. On the other hand, it could have prevented the referendums from being diverted away from their real objective by opportunistic political leaders and by voters eager to cast a "protest vote" against their national governments for essentially domestic reasons.

Such a coordinated effort proved impossible, however, owing to the breakdown at the summit of Brussels on 13 December 2003 and to the prudence of the Irish Presidency, which sought to avoid rushing the negotiations. In June of 2004, the European elections were marked by record levels of abstention in most Member

States, and campaigns nearly everywhere focused on issues almost exclusively of national significance. Ironically, these inward-looking campaigns were carried out just as the work of the IGC was gearing up again for the adoption of a Constitution transcending national politics.

On 20 April 2004, British Prime Minister Tony Blair unexpectedly announced the intention of the government to hold a referendum on the Constitution. Even before the summit of 18 June 2004, other governments followed the UK's example, in some cases without investigating whether such a referendum was consistent with their own constitutions and without specifying whether or not the referendum would be binding, although from a political and practical point of view even consultative referendums can be determinative. Since then, many if not most observers have predicted that it will be impossible for the ratification process to succeed in all of the twenty-five Member States given the numerous foreseen referendums. Already by the beginning of the summer of 2004, plans to hold such referendums were announced not only by the UK but also by Denmark, France, Ireland, Luxembourg, Portugal and Spain. Similar announcements were later made by the Czech Republic, The Netherlands and Poland, while as of March 2005, it appeared that a referendum might also be a possibility in Finland. On 20 February 2005, Spain asserted itself as the first link in the chain of popular votes, with a relatively low turnout (43%) but a very positive endorsement (nearly 77%) of the Constitution. Meanwhile, ratification limited to a parliamentary vote has already succeeded in Austria, Greece, Hungary, Italy, Latvia, Lithuania, Slovakia, Slovenia, and similar votes will be taken in Belgium, Cyprus, Estonia, Germany, Malta, and Sweden. The idea of holding a referendum in all of the Member States on the same date might have seemed appealing but could easily have backfired, providing ammunition to those arguing that Brussels interferes in everything, even in the date of a national referendum.

Rather than attempting to predict the future, it may be observed that no one had announced in public or foresaw the obstacles to ratification which have manifested themselves since 1980. In 1986, a certain Mr Crotty decided to bring proceedings before the Supreme Court of Ireland to challenge the ratification of the Single European Act, which delayed its entry into force until six months after the date the Treaty had provided for. In 1992, Danish voters rejected the ratification of the Maastricht Treaty in June, and the French nearly did the same in September. This effectively frustrated the timely entry into force of that Treaty, which had been scheduled for 1 January 1993. A new referendum in Denmark had positive results, but in Germany, a Mr Brünner challenged Germany's ratification before the Federal Constitutional Court. Consequently, the Treaty could not enter into force until 1 November 1993. In 1998, despite expectations of a negative outcome in the Danish referendum on the Treaty of Amsterdam, the results of the vote – conducted in a general climate of apathy – were actually quite positive. Nevertheless, the overall ratification process had to wait for the Flemish component of the Regional

Parliament of Brussels, which, following votes by the six other assemblies whose assent is necessary under the Belgian Constitution, finally decided to authorise ratification. The Treaty of Amsterdam thus took effect on 1 May 1999.

In 2001, without any warning, the Irish electorate – considered to be fervently pro-European – abstained *en masse* in a referendum on the Treaty of Nice. The low turnout effectively precluded a sufficient number of "yeas" for the referendum to pass, which had significant consequences: the Treaty's entry into force was a prerequisite to the signing of the Treaty of Accession between the Union and the ten candidate countries waiting to become Member States. Another year elapsed before a new referendum permitted the government to ratify the Treaty, which entered into force on 1 February 2003, during the most intense period of the European Convention and little more than a month before the Act of Enlargement was signed.

In 1974, under the leadership of Harold Wilson, the Labour government won the elections in the UK. At that time, the Labour party was largely hostile to the participation of the UK in the European Community, which the country had effectively joined on 1 January 1973. One of the reasons for Wilson's victory was undoubtedly the fact that he had promised to launch a referendum to be voted on by a public which, according to polls, was strongly opposed to the Common Market. Yet the non-binding referendum, held in June of 1975, in fact indicated a broad majority favouring the UK's membership in the Community.

In 2003, many observers expected the Treaty of Accession to be rejected in referendums in at least some of the ten candidate countries, much as a similar treaty had been rejected in Norway in 1972 and as Swiss voters in 1992 had rejected Switzerland's participation in the EEA. Indeed, many of the ten candidate countries had constitutional provisions conditioning the validity of such referendums on a high level of turnout at the polls, which made the fate of the Treaty of Accession still less certain.

However, ratification of the Treaty of Accession, which in the end was of course successfully achieved in all ten of the new Member States, is not quite as precarious as ratification of a Treaty – in this case, the Constitution – which revises earlier Treaties of the Union. If a country fails to ratify a Treaty of Accession, this only prevents the entry into the Union of the country in question; it does not affect the entry of other acceding countries. For Treaties of revision, the matter is much less simple. Clearly, such a Treaty cannot enter into force if it is not ratified by all of the Member States. However, the consequences of a failure by one or more countries to ratify the Treaty are not easy to predict, and much will depend on factors such as the precise wording of the question presented to voters. The Portuguese Constitutional Court examined this issue in 1998, when the national government sought to submit the Treaty of Amsterdam to a referendum embodied in the following question: "Do you approve of the continuing participation of Portugal in the construction of the European Union within the framework of the

Treaty of Amsterdam?" The Constitutional Court held that the formulation of the question was unconstitutionally imprecise, as a voter would not have known with sufficient certainty whether he was being asked for his opinion on the Treaty as such or on the continuing membership of Portugal in the Union. A similar problem arose with respect to the planned Portuguese referendum on the Constitution. The question that would have been posed to the voters ("Do you agree with the Charter of Fundamental Rights, the qualified majority voting (QMV) rule and the new institutional framework of the European Union, as established in the Constitution for Europe?") was condemned by the Constitutional Court in December of 2004 as being open to multiple interpretations. In addition to the manner in which the referendums on the Constitution are phrased, their success will also obviously depend on the electoral campaign conducted in each of the relevant Member States and the degree to which voters consider themselves sufficiently informed as to the contents and significance of the text. Ideally, the voters' position on the project of European integration will in the end influence the results of the referendums more than the popularity of the national governments that happen to be in power. In any event, regardless of whether the yeas or the nays prevail, the outcome should be seen as a victory for the democratisation of the construction of Europe.

2.2. To be Continued . . .

Article IV-447(2) of the Constitution provides:

> This Treaty shall enter into force on 1 November 2006, provided that all the instruments of ratification have been deposited, or, failing that, on the first day of the second month following the deposit of the instrument of ratification by the last signatory State to take this step.

The Convention's text already made reference, in a final declaration, to the possibility of a failure in the ratification process. The Praesidium had originally proposed to incorporate the relevant provision in the Article concerning the Constitution's entry into force, but this drew opposition from certain representatives of the national governments. It was therefore necessary to resort to the inclusion of a "Declaration".

Final Act of the Intergovernmental Conference

Declaration on the Ratification of the Treaty Establishing a Constitution for Europe

The Conference notes that if, two years after the signature of the Treaty establishing a Constitution for Europe, four fifths of the Member States have ratified it and one or more Member States have encountered difficulties in proceeding with ratification, the matter will be referred to the European Council.

Many commentators have prognosticated on the portents of this Declaration, which was adopted by the IGC. From a legal point of view, it has no meaning at all, except that the European Council would be obliged to discuss the problem if, by 1 November 2006 (envisaged by Article IV-447 as the date on which the Constitution would enter into force), a certain number of Member States failed to ratify the text. From a political point of view, it is clear that the consequences will depend on whether one or more Member States have failed to ratify it, which ones they are, and – if the failure to ratify is due to a referendum rejected by voters – the question posed, the number of abstentions and the relationship between affirmative and negative votes. Out of respect for democracy, both a modification of the text and a complementary protocol would then have to be negotiated – a measure that was not taken following either Denmark's "no" in 1991 or Ireland's "no" in 2003. The critical question would be whether such a negotiation could be limited to points of detail, or whether the entire settlement reached by the Convention and the IGC would be subject to renewed examination.

Referendums were held in France and The Netherlands on 29 May and 1 June 2005. It was agreed that, whatever the results of these referendums, the ratification process would continue. In the event, a majority of French voters rejected ratification, and the Dutch voters did the same.

The European Council, at its meeting of 16 June, decided that those Member States wishing to proceed immediately with their ratification procedure could go ahead while others could wait for a change of political climate. The British government had already decided, on 6 June, to postpone the foreseen UK referendum. The precedents of Denmark in relation to the Maastricht Treaty in 1992–1993 and of Ireland in connection with Nice Treaty in 2001–2002 show that if a government is able to win back the electorate's confidence, it is possible to proceed to a new referendum – with good prospects of a positive outcome – on a previously submitted treaty, accompanied by a new text that does not have the characteristics of a treaty and therefore needs no ratification by other Member States (for example, a declaration of the European Council). As in Ireland in 2002, this new referendum may also be voted on contemporaneously with an amendment the national Constitution.

A provision analogous to the Declaration on ratification was contained in Article 99 of the Coal and Steel Treaty, but it did not prove necessary to apply it. On the other hand, the Treaty establishing the European Defence Community (EDC), signed in Paris on 27 May 1952, never entered into force. On 10 March 1953, an *Ad Hoc* Assembly appointed by the original six Member States approved a "Draft Treaty Embodying the Statute of the European Community", the fruit of a Franco-Italian initiative, which would have established a European Political Community. On 19 March, Germany ratified the draft EDC Treaty, and in the following six months the three Benelux countries followed suit. On 22 September 1953, a conference of foreign ministers meeting in Rome noted differences relating to the supranational aspects of the proposed European Political Community.

On 30 August 1954, the French *Assemblée nationale* refused to discuss the EDC Treaty, and no one will ever know whether among the deputies there was in fact a majority opposed to the text. Since the European Political Community was directly linked to certain provisions in the EDC Treaty, the death of the latter also necessarily dispatched the former. Yet this was a temporary setback: two and a half years later in Messina, the representatives of France, Germany, Italy and the Benelux countries agreed on what was to become the first Treaty of Rome.

RELATED READING

The following selections should be regarded as a point of departure and are by no means exhaustive.

AMATO G. AND BRIBOSIA H. (gen. eds.), *Quelle charte constitutionelle pour l'Union europèenne?* – *Strategies et options pour renforcer le caractère constitutionnel des traités – Etude de l'Institut Universitaire Européen*, Luxembourg, European Parliament, *Politique poli* series 105A, FR, 1998.

BASSANINI F. AND TIBERI G. (gen. eds.), *Una Costituzione per l'Europa. Dalla Convenzione europa alla Conferenza intergovernativa*, Pubblicazioni Astrid, Bologna, Il Mulino, 2003.

BELLAMY R. AND CASTIGLIONE D., *Legitimizing the Euro-'Polity' and its 'Regime' – the Normative Turn in EU Studies*, 2(1) European Journal of Political Theory 7-34, 2003.

BIFULCO R., CARTABIA M. AND CELOTTO A. (gen. eds.), *l'Europa dei diritti – Commento alla Carta dei diritti fondamentali dell'Unione europea*, Bologna, Il Mulino, 2001.

BLANKART C. AND MUELLER D. (gen. eds.), *A Constitution for the European Union (CESifo Seminar Series)*, Cambridge, MA, The MIT Press, 2004.

BORGAN G. (gen. ed.), *Il modello sociale nella Costituzione europea*, Bologna, Il Mulino, 2004.

BRAIBANT G., *La Charte des droits fondamentaux de l'Union europèenne*, Paris, Seuil, 2001.

CASSESE S., *La Costituzione europea*, in "Quaderni costituzionali", no. 3, p. 487, December 1991; *La "Costituzione" europea del 1957 comparata con quella ora in preparazione*, in "Giornale di diritto amministrativo", no. 8, p. 867, August 2003; and *L'integrazione attraverso il diritto: equilibrio dei poteri e legitimazione nella nuova Unione europea*, in "Giornale di diritto amministrativo", no. 8, p. 871, August 2003.

CIDE, *Una costituzione per la nuova Europa*, progetto di trattato, Milan, Giuffrè, 2003.

CRAIG P., *Constitutions, Constitutionalism and the EU*, 7(2) European Law Journal 125-150, 2001.

CRAIG P., *The Constitutional Treaty: Legislative and Executive Power in the Emerging Constitutional Order*, EUI Working Paper (Law) no. 7, Florence, European University Institute, 2004.

CURTIN D., GRILLER S., PRECHAL S. AND DE WITTE B. (gen. eds.), *The Emerging Constitution of the European Union*, Oxford, Oxford University Press, 2004.

DE BURCA G., *The Constitutional Challenge of New Governance in the European Union*, 28(6) European Law Review 814-839, 2003.

DE BURCA G., SCOTT J., TWINING W. (series ed.) AND MCCRUDDEN C. (series ed.), *Constitution of the European Union (Law in Context)*, Cambridge, Cambridge University Press, 2004.

DE WITTE B., *Simplification and Reorganization of the European Treaties*, 39(6) Common Market Law Review, 1255-1287, 2002.

DE WITTE, B. (gen. ed.), *Ten reflections on the Constitutional Treaty of Europe*, Florence, European University Institute, 2003.

DOBSON L. AND FOLLESDAL A. (gen. eds.), *Political Theory and the European Constitution (Routledge/Ecpr Studies in European Political Science)*, London and New York, Routledge, 2004.

DOUGAN M., DASHWOOD A., HILLION C., SPAVENTA E. AND JOHNSTON A., *Draft Constitutional Treaty of the European Union and Related Documents*, 28(1) European Law Review 763-793, 2003.

EECKHOUT P., *The EU-Charter of Fundamental Rights and the Federal Question*, 39(5) Common Market Law Review 945-994, 2002.

Related Reading

EHLERMANN C.-D., MENY Y. AND BRIBOSIA H. (gen. eds.), *A basic treaty for the European Union: A study of the reorganisation of the Treaties*, presented to European President Romano Prodi on 15 May 2000, Florence, European University Institute, 2000

EHLERMANN C.-D., MENY Y. AND BRIBOSIA H. (gen. eds.), Reforming the Treaties' amendment procedures: Second report on the reorganisation of the European Union Treaties, presented to the European Commission on 31 July 2000, Florence, European University Institute, 2000.

ERIKSEN E., FOSSUM J. AND MENÉNDEZ A., *Developing a Constitution for Europe*, London and New York, Routledge, 2004.

GERBET P., DE LA SERRE F. AND NAFILYAN G., *L'Union politique de l'Europe – Jalons et textes*, Paris, La Documentation Française, « Retour au texte », 1998.

GOWAN P. AND ANDERSEN P. (gen. eds.), *The Question of Europe*, London and New York, Verso, 1997.

GREWE C. AND OBERDORFF, H., *Les Constitutions de États de l'Union européenne*, Paris, La Documentation Française, « Retour au texte », 1999.

HALBERSTAM D., *The Bride of Messina or European Democracy and the Limits of Liberal Intergovernmentalism*, in Eisgruber P. and Weiler J.H.H. (gen. eds.), Altneuland: The EU Constitution in a Contextual Perspective, *Jean Monnet Working Papers no. 5*, 2004.

JACOBS F., *The Evolution of the European Legal Order*, 41(2) Common Market Law Review 303-316, 2004.

JACQUÉ, JEAN-PAUL, *The Principle of Institutional Balance*, 41(2) Common Market Law Review 383-391, 2004.

JOERGES C. MÉNY Y. AND WEILER J.H.H. (gen. eds.), *What Kind of Constitution for What Kind of Polity: Responses to Joschka Fischer*, Florence, Robert Schuman Centre for Advanced Studies, European University Institute, 2000.

LENAERTS K. AND DESOMER M., *Bricks for a Constitutional Treaty of the European Union: Values, Objectives and Means*, 27(4) European Law Review, 377-407, 2002.

LENAERTS K. AND GERARD D., *The Structure of the Union According to the Constitution for Europe: The Emperor is Getting Dressed*, 29(3) European Law Review 289-322, 2004.

MANCINI F., *Democracy and constitutionalism in the European Union: collected essays*, Oxford, Hart, 2000.

MONNET J., *Mémoires*, Paris, Fayard, 1976.

MONNET J., *Memoirs* (English translation), Garden City, Doubleday, 1978.

NORMAN P., *The Accidental Constitution: The Story of the European Convention*, Lancaster, Gazelle, 2003.

PASQUINUCCI D., *I progetti di costituzione europea dall'Assemblea "ad hoc" alla Dichiarazione di Laeken*, Milan, Unicopli, 2003.

PERNICE I., *Multilevel Constitutionalism in the European Union*, 27(5) European Law Review 511-529, 2002.

PHINNEMORE D. AND CHURCH C., *Understanding the European Constitution*, London and New York, Routledge, 2005.

ROSSI L.S. (gen. ed.), *Il progetto di Trattato-Costituzione. Verso una nuova architettura dell'Unione europea*, Milano, Giuffré, 2004.

POIARES MADURO M., *How Constitutional Can the European Union Be? The Tension Between Intergovernmentalism and Constitutionalism in the European Union*, in Eisgruber P. and Weiler J.H.H. (gen. eds.), Altneuland: The EU Constitution in a Contextual Perspective, *Jean Monnet Working Papers no. 5*, 2004.

PONZANO P., *La réforme des Institutions de l'Union européenne dans le cadre de la Constitution*, Revue du droit de l'Union européenne, no. 1, 25-38, 2004.

162

SHAW J., *Process, Responsibility and Inclusion in EU Constitutionalism*, 9(1) European Law Journal 45-68, 2003.

SHAW J., *The Convention on the Future of Europe. Working towards an EU Constitution*, London, Editions Kogan Page, 2003.

SPINI V., *Alla convenzione europea: diario e documenti da Bruxelles. Con il testo integrale del progetto di Costituzione*, Florence, Alinea, 2003.

STEIN E., *Lawyers, Judges and the Making of a Transnational Constitution*, 75(1) American Journal of International Law 1-27, 1981.

TIZZANO A. (gen. ed.), *Una costituzione per l'Europa. Testi e documenti relativi alla Convenzione europea*, Milano, Giuffrè, 2004.

TONIATTI R. (gen. ed.), *La Carta dei diritti fondamentali dell'Unione europea*, Padova, Cedam, 2002.

TRECHSEL A., *How to Federalize the Union . . . and Why Bother*, Journal of European Public Policy (special issue), 2005.

WALKER N., *Constitutionalising Enlargement, Enlarging Constitutionalism*, 9(3) European Law Journal 365-385, 2003.

WALKER N., *Europe's Constitutional Momentum and the Search for Polity Legitimacy*, in Eisgruber P. and Weiler J.H.H. (gen. eds.), Altneuland: The EU Constitution in a Contextual Perspective, *Jean Monnet Working Papers no. 5*, 2004.

WEILER, J.H.H., *The Constitution of Europe – 'Do the New Clothes Have an Emperor?' and other Essays on European Integration*, Cambridge, Cambridge University Press, 1999.

WEILER J.H.H. AND WIND M. (gen. eds.), *European Constitutionalism Beyond the State*, Cambridge, Cambridge University Press, 2003.

ZILLER J. (gen. ed.), *L'européanisation des droits constitutionnels à la lumière de la Constitution pour l'Europe – The Europeanisation of Constitutional Law in the Light of the Constitution for Europe*, Paris, L'Harmattan, 2003.